CLOSE UPS &

CLOSE ENCOUNTERS

A VIEW FROM BEHIND THE LENS

BY

S. J. BROWN

Close Ups & Close Encounters

Published by Acorn Book Services

sjbrown.pictures@hotmail.com

Designed by Acorn Book Services

Publication Managed by Acorn Book Services
www.acornbookservices.com
acorn.book.services@comcast.net
304-285-8205

Cover designed by Todd Aune
Spokane, Washington
www.projetoonline.com

Cover Image: S.J. Brown

ISBN-10: 0985726784
ISBN-13: 978-0-9857267-8-2

Published in the United States of America

This book is dedicated to Nature Lovers every where.

With special thanks to Jay, Corinne, family, friends and the members of "The Group".

Close Ups &

Close Encounters

A View From Behind The Lens

INTRODUCTION

The life of a wildlife photographer is quite different than most people imagine. There is much more to it than simply having a camera and a sense of adventure. I didn't realize just how it would impact both my life, and the lives of those around me. I just thought it would be exciting and fun.

My interactions with animals—some friendly, some not—are all detailed within these pages. Whether looking an alligator in the eye or quietly observing a small bird for me there is always a sense of wonder and a connection with the world around us.

I have chosen to be a freelance photographer, this gives me the option of photographing the wildlife I choose; however my income is sporadic. The variety of locations I access are primarily public lands accessible to anyone, so readers can search for these animals as well.

Thirty-five millimeter film is my chosen medium. When viewing my photographs you see what I saw through the lens. The stories within these pages will help you experience my encounters. Come along as I go into the homes of a variety of wild animals and bring the experience into your home.

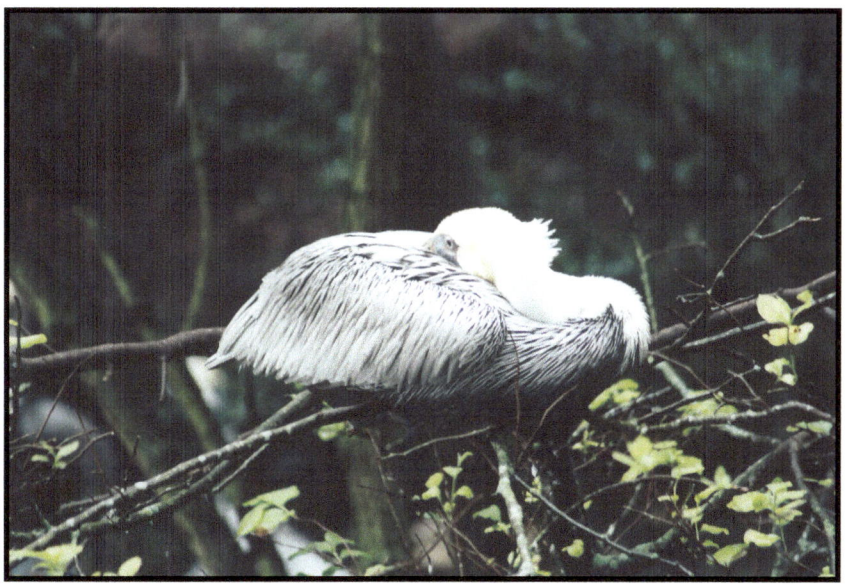

S.J. Brown

TABLE OF CONTENTS

A Crazy Idea..10

Venturing Out...14

Captive Critters..18

Nationally Interesting...22

Hoofing It..26

Got Any Bobcat Photographs?...30

Prehistoric Encounters..34

Snowy Adventures..38

Bearly Red...42

Feathers, Fur, and Scales...46

The Playful Pachyderm..50

Camping Out..54

Photographic Memories...60

A New Project..64

River Excursion..68

Picturing a Few Birds..74

Lost...78

Northern Expedition...82

To The Rescue..86

Going Solo...90

Knot Crabby..94

A Wild Ride...98

Following Feathers..102

This Place is for the Birds..108

Message from S. J. Brown...112

A Crazy Idea

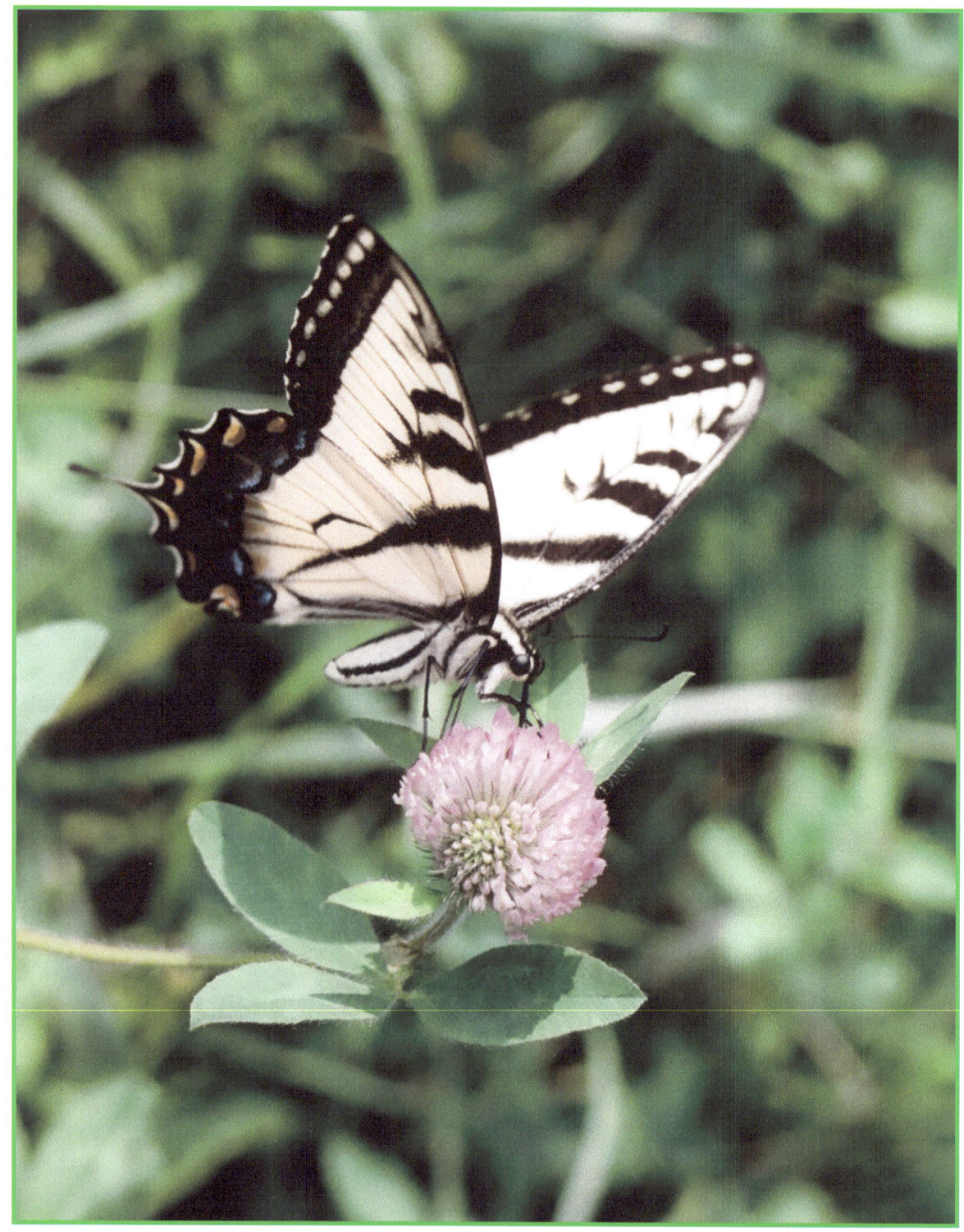

The eerie sound of the foghorn echoed through the thick mist that surrounded us. Skillfully, our captain maneuvered the boat out of the harbor toward the open ocean.

He was a stout man with long gray hair and a thick beard. His love of the sea was obvious as he stood at the helm. He spoke with an air of authority as he assured us he could find the island even in this thick fog.

His first mate was a tall, thin, high school student who shared the Captain's love of the sea. Together they had safely transported national magazine and newspaper photographers. This boat and its crew had been trusted with politicians, birdwatchers, and tourist to various locations. Surely they could get us to our destination and back.

Since I can't swim, being on a boat wasn't my favorite place to be. I sat nervously with my hand tightly gripping the top rail of the boat. The roughness of the seas added to my anxiety. Not having my feet planted firmly on the ground always made me nervous.

As the waves crashed into the sides of the boat, I glanced to my right. There, intently scanning the fog for any signs of life, was Jay. He is my extra pair of eyes, my spotter, my husband, my driver, and my safety net. His large build, full thick beard, and curly head of dark hair are always topped off by a baseball cap, worn with the brim turned to the back. His customary worn out jeans and work boots add to his rugged appearance. Under this tough exterior hides a quick wit, a heart of gold, an unexpected gentleness, and an impatient 5 year old. He looked over at me and smiled.

Peering out into the thick fog over the sea, my mind wondered back to how this all began.

After a hectic day, I slumped down on the couch to watch a little television and enjoy some dinner. Across the room Jay remote in hand, scanned the venue of possible choices. He decided to see what the public broadcasting station had to offer.

"Tonight, we will hear from a variety of wildlife photographers. We are going to get a glimpse into their not so typical lives. You'll see just what it takes to get close to wildlife and get that perfect shot that may one day grace the cover of a national magazine."

"Interesting," I thought.

Our eyes were fixed on the television, savoring every moment of the show. I envied those photographers being outdoors close to wildlife, and, I assumed, getting paid for it. All too soon the show was over. Little did we know that one television show would change our lives so dramatically.

Despite a very tight budget, a child in college, bills to pay, and a business to run, Jay was slowly convincing me I should embark on a new career.

He argued that all I needed was a decent camera and a few rolls of film. I could start right here in the backyard. There were birds, butterflies, squirrels, and ground hogs.

Within days, I had a new camera, a few rolls of film, and I was about to get the education of my life. I soon discovered there is a big difference between seeing animals and photographing them. Over the next few weeks, I was in the backyard photographing critters whenever I could. I was discovering different shutter speeds and settings that the camera offered. I was taking the time to get vertical shots, as well as horizontal ones.

By turning the camera sideways, I could photograph an entire bird, including his tail and still zoom in on his face.

In some cultures, when you take a person's picture, they believe you take a piece of the subject's soul. Others believe that the eyes are the windows to the soul. When I photograph animals, I want them to look right into the lens and allow me to take their photograph. I would zoom in close enough to look into the eyes of a squirrel while photographing it. By looking into the eyes of an animal, I may be getting a glimpse of their essence.

This is when my love of face shots began. I want the person viewing the photograph to be able to actually look into the eyes of the animal in the picture.

I preferred shooting straight at the subject of the photograph and not at an angle. This meant that if I was photographing a bird in a tree, I had to get up in the air. The front porch roof proved to be just the right height to get photographs of the birds at one of the feeders. I would crawl out the bedroom window and sit on the porch roof after filling the feeder. Once the birds arrived for their meal, I would click away.

Soon I discovered that my experiments with photography were a source of amusement for one of my neighbors. On sunny afternoons, Rita would sit on her porch to see what I was up to that day. The angle of our houses and the curve in the road allowed her to view most of our yard. She would watch me standing on the roof of Jay's truck, or on the picnic table to photograph a bird in a tree. She would chuckle as I lay on the ground under the car or a bush to get a picture of a turtle, or perhaps a snake in the grass.

Right from the beginning, Jay was by my side, spotting critters and coaxing me on. A butterfly passing through the yard became one of my first targets. With my camera in hand, I slowly crept up on my winged subject.

"Hello there, want your picture taken?" I whispered.

Just as I was within camera range, the butterfly departed from his perch. He was enticed by the sweet nectar of the colorful flowers across the yard. When the butterfly landed on one of the bright yellow blooms, I approached while watching it intently. Closer and closer I ventured across the lawn still wet with the morning dew. Suddenly, I slipped and stubbed my toe. I landed face first in the midst of the flowers, and the butterfly flew away.

Jay laughed so hard that he had to sit down.

After examining my bloody knee, I brushed myself off and glanced about the yard in search of the illusive butterfly. From over my shoulder, his graceful wings approached. The stark black lines that framed his wings glistened in the sun when he once again landed in the flower garden.

Cautiously this time, I approached him. As I raised the camera to my face, the butterfly transferred to another flower. I watched him through the lens, and slowly repositioned myself. As I depressed the shutter button, it was obvious the camera wasn't turned on.

While turning on the camera, my gaze was distracted by the butterfly venturing to another flower. His delicate wings gently brushed the blooms when he floated by. Peering through the lens I adjusted my position and bumped into a tree. Of course, the butterfly flew away.

I saw Jay across the yard shaking his head and cackling.

More determined than ever to get a photograph, I continued the chase. There, back at the very same bush where this all started, the butterfly landed. I carefully stepped between the flowers, raised the camera to my face, held my breath and pressed the shutter button.

"I think I got him, I think I got him."

Jay's response was "Are you sure?"

This led to another hour of pursuit, but eventually I finished off my first roll of film. When I examined the pictures, there was a blurred shot of a squirrel that had moved as I clicked the shutter button. A shot of the tail of a bird that flew off just a second too soon was next. Several shots included no animals at all, just the tree or bush they left behind. Dark, shadowy pictures were scattered throughout the roll.

Then, I came to a shot of the illusive butterfly. It was a simple image, but upon examining it, the black coloring on the butterfly was a stark contrast to the bright pink of the flower it was visiting. The image was crisp and quite clear. I could actually see its legs and antenna. The black and yellow coloring that adorned its wings blended into the picture beautifully.

I was hooked.

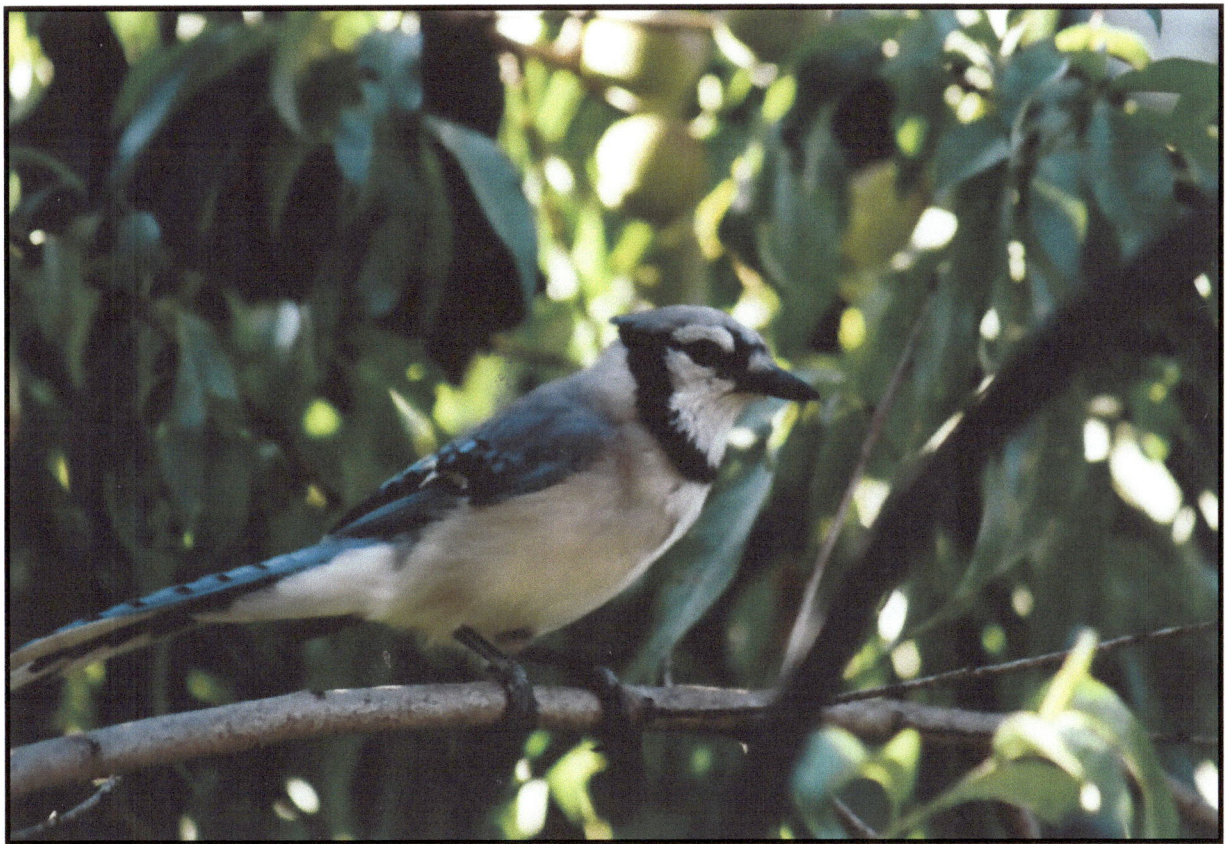

Venturing Out

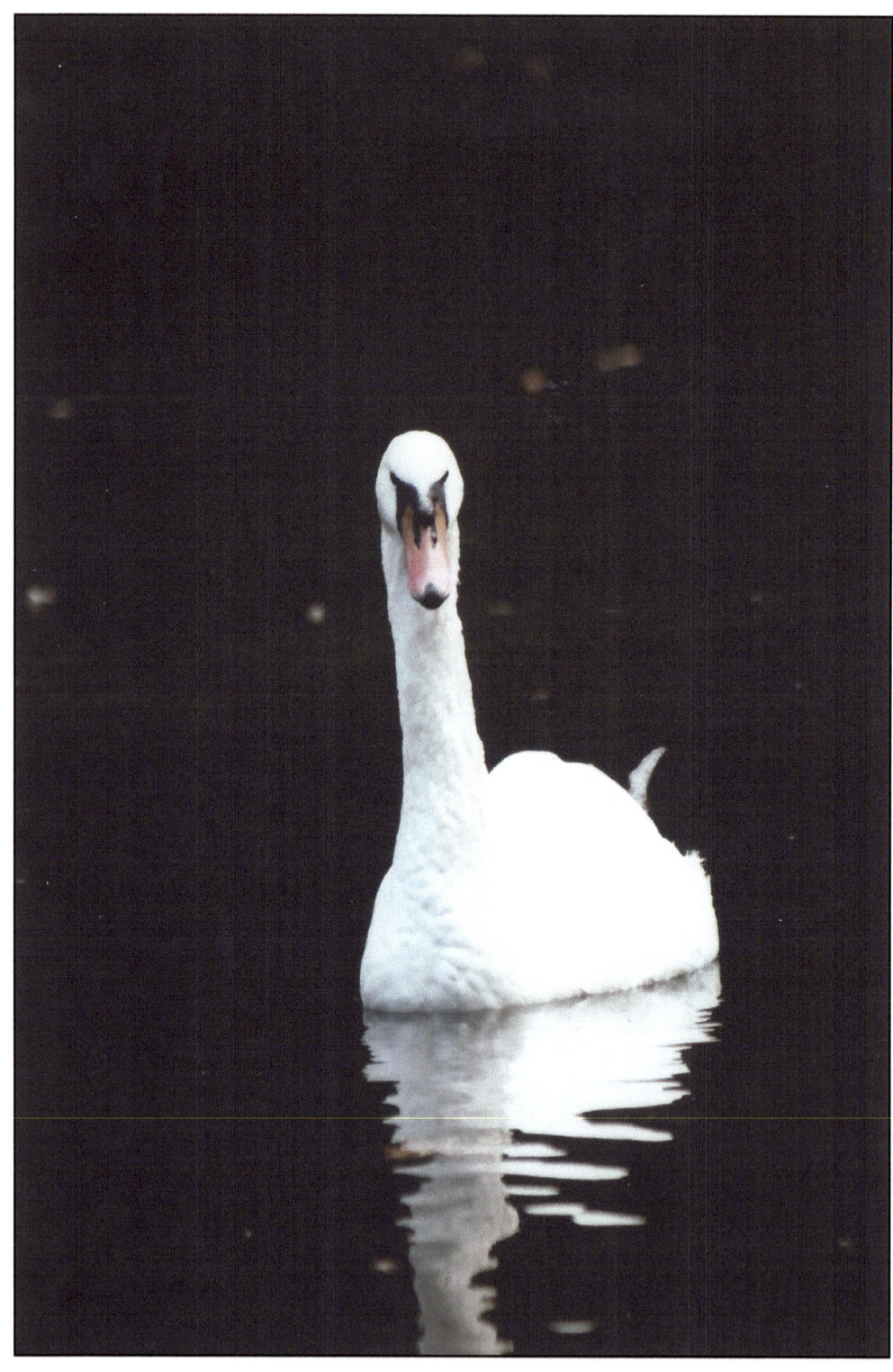

The areas around where most people live are a goldmine for photographic opportunities. Public lands work out well for taking in the scenic splendor of the landscape, and often offer the opportunity to observe wildlife. I had heard a nearby park was filled with ducks and geese, along with a variety of songbirds. It was a warm, sunny day, so a visit to the park sounded like a great idea. I was thrilled with the notion of venturing out to take pictures in a totally new environment.

The short drive to the park seemed endless. After getting lost a few times, we finally arrived. The traffic on the nearby streets seemed to disappear after we entered the park through the decorative archway. There was activity everywhere; honks and quacks filled the air while ducks and geese wandered among the many people visiting the park.

Since people were in the habit of feeding the water fowl, they had become accustomed to humans. This gave me the opportunity to get quite close to them. I was taking a minute to survey the area, when a lone duck waddled toward me. Kneeling down, I gazed through the lens, and my index finger quivered as I slowly depressed the shutter button.

I was close enough to capture the texture of the dark feathers that adorned the male mallard's neck. I was able to look into his dark soulful eyes and click off another frame. Minutes later, I zoomed in on a goose and had its head fill the entire lens.

Near the playground area, children's laughter filled the air.

Further down the path, I saw flocks of geese and ducks. Using a tree to block the birds' view of me, I crept closer and crouched down to get a shot of a pair of snow geese nesting on the ground.

After capturing them on film, I found myself face to face with a Canada goose. His pitch black eye studied me as I focused in on the subtle hook at the end of his beak. The click of the camera startled him, and he waddled off quickly flapping his wings as he went.

Surprised, I tumbled to the ground, giggling.

Then, in one of the many ponds, I watched a goose splash about happily in the cool water. I adjusted the shutter speed a bit and tried to get this moment on film when I spied a mockingbird in a bush nearby. Its high pitched melody echoed in the air.

I slowly approached. Just as I raised my camera, the mockingbird flew off. I caught a glimpse of the fine white feathers of his underbelly as he glided out of view.

Jay spied a swan quietly floating along the water's edge. We walked closer to the water.

Careful not to scare this elegant creature, I sat down slowly and snapped a picture of the swan as it approached.

Then, it decided to join me on the shore. Once out of the water, he seemed quite clumsy and awkward. His large, black feet smacked the ground as he walked. He waddled from side to side, honking and demanding food as he proceeded.

I managed to get a few close-up shots of him during his approach. Focusing the camera proved to be challenging due to the subtle breeze playing with the delicate white feathers.

Once he discovered I didn't have any food for him, the swan returned to the water and drifted to the other side of the pond.

There were numerous secluded wooded areas to explore. There was a mallard here, a Canada goose there. The biggest challenge seemed to be deciding which one of the animals to photograph. While I was photographing one animal, Jay would be pointing out another close by. I was able to capture a few on land and others in the water.

As I looked through the lens, the couple conversing on a nearby bench seemed to fade away.

The large black feet on a baby duck seemed out of place as it moved closer. I focused in on the dark fluffy down covering its body, as it was caressed by the breeze. I was now lying on the ground, savoring the image in the lens. A sudden quack from Mom startled both of us sending the duckling scurrying off, and the moment was gone.

I turned to find two curious geese to my left. Startled, I scooted back a bit, trying to get them focused in the lens. One of the geese abruptly pecked at the camera. The next few minutes were a series of pecks, clicks, giggles, and honks until I used up the film that was in the camera.

"Okay, guys. The fun's over, I have to reload."

I stood up and brushed myself off as the pair quietly wandered away. They seemed to be disappointed that the game was over.

Jay and I followed a narrow path that led to a small secluded pond. There, we spied a pitch black bird with a white beak and bright red eyes. We noticed the bird's yellow legs paddling just below the surface of the water. The bird didn't seem to be as comfortable around people as the ducks and geese were. I sat quietly to let it get used to my presence. Eventually, it floated toward me, and I captured it on film. I snapped off several frames before leaving the lone bird drifting quietly along in the afternoon sun. I had a few good shots of him.

I would later identify the mystery bird as a coot.

As we made our way back to the parking area, Jay and I were greeted by a flock of snow geese. Their wide, white bodies perched on bright, orange legs quickly approached. We were soon surrounded by the group of honking geese demanding food. Their large feet slapped in the mud while we slowly crept toward the truck. Frantically, they pecked at the camera bag in hopes of getting a morsel or two.

"Back off, guys, I don't have any food," Jay shouted.

"Get off my foot, you silly bird," I said.

The flock soon spotted some newcomers to the park carrying bags, and they dashed off to investigate. Jay and I ran for the truck while they were distracted. We decided to come back here again over the winter, to get some shots of the birds in the snow. We also planned to bring some food for them next time.

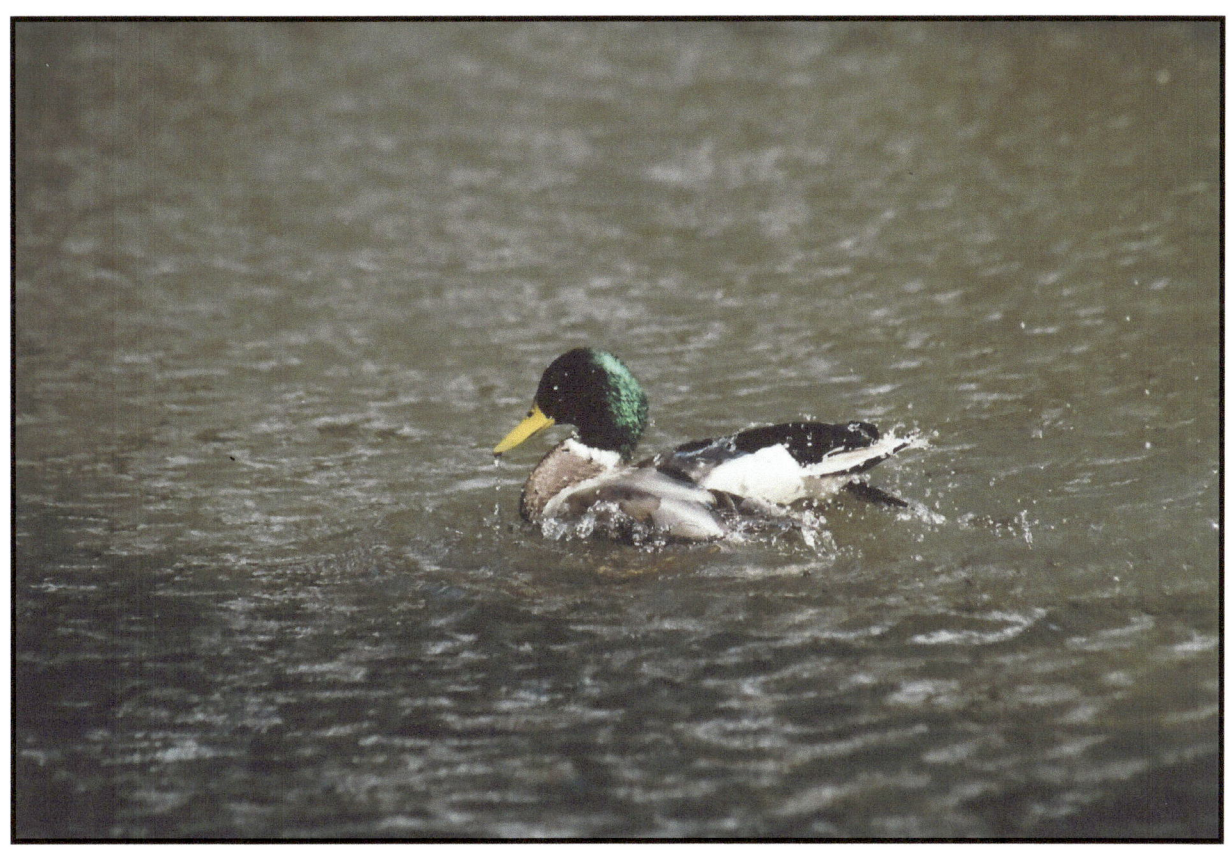

CAPTIVE CRITTERS

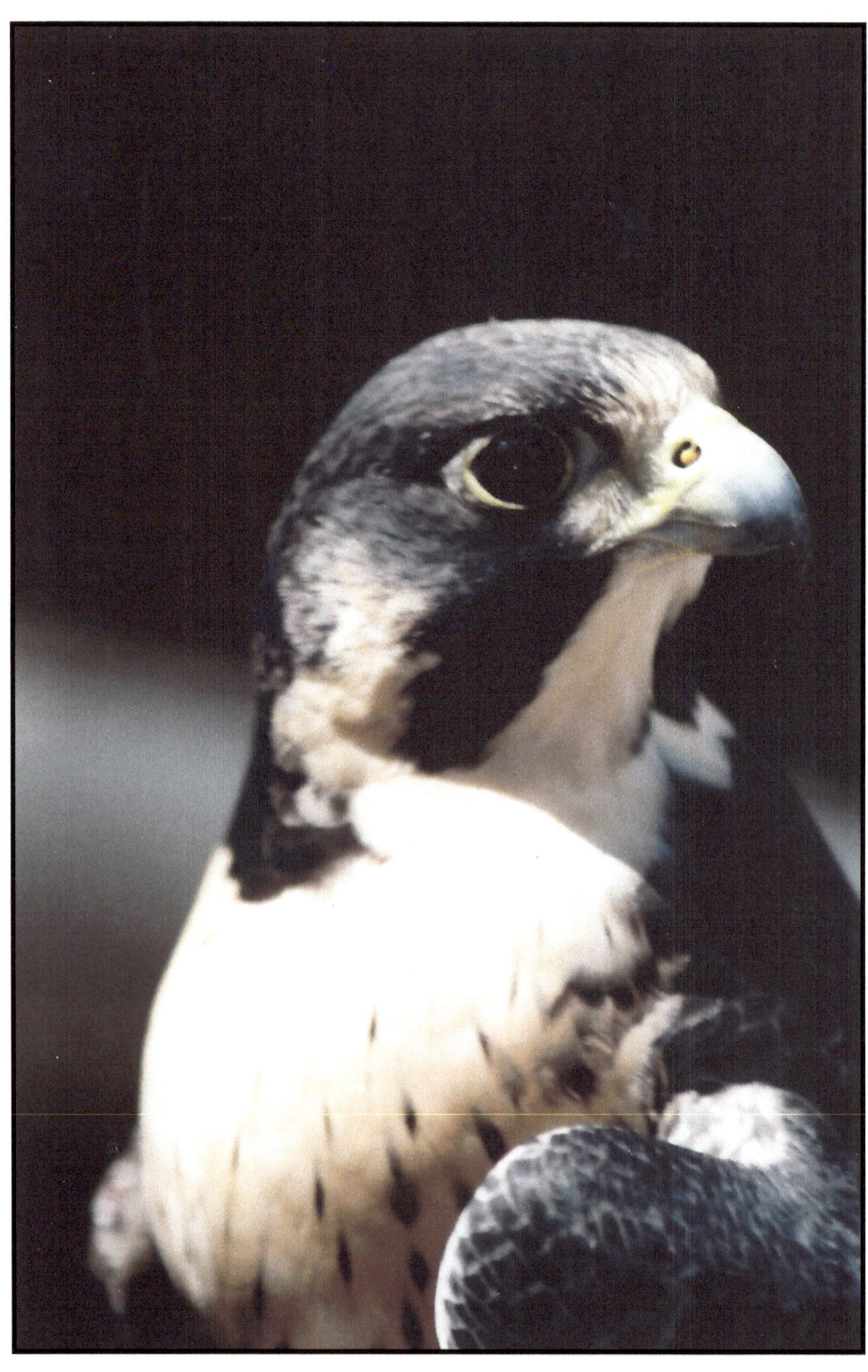

Generally speaking, working with a wildlife photographer as a spotter is a rather safe job. Spotters seek out wild animals, or critters as I call them, and stand back. Without one, a wildlife photographer simply couldn't function effectively. A spotter proves their worth every time they point out an animal the photographer didn't see. My spotter, Jay has spent years honing his spotting skills. Even in dark shadows or blinding sunlight he can tell the type of bird we are looking at by the shape of its wings or the way it is perched. His keen eyes notice the slightest movement even in deep underbrush. He keeps me out of harm's way by watching my back. In our case, Jay is not only my spotter, but my compass as well, since I have no sense of direction.

On the rare occasions I don't need a spotter, he offers helpful advice on angles and holds some of my equipment. This was the case on a sunny afternoon when I was photographing some captive animals.

A rugged path led us from one enclosure to another. These were animals that had been injured in some way and could not survive in the wild. Since they were fed by people, our presence didn't seem to disturb them.

I framed in a very intimidating looking Turkey Vulture. His massive body was covered with delicate black feathers that reflected in the afternoon sun. These were topped off by his wrinkled forehead.

As we wandered, a lone Canada goose followed behind us honking, and probably looking for a handout. While most of the inhabitants were birds, there was a beautiful red fox tucked off in a corner enclosure. He was clothed in subtle rust, white, black, and gray fur. Basking in the sun, he made a wonderful picture and was quite cooperative as I clicked away.

On another occasion, I was invited to photograph some captive critters that were once considered pets. I had zoomed in on a variety of creatures throughout the day, but upon the advice of the animals' caretaker, we had left the tigers until last.

There were two of them: one male, one female. They each had their own enclosure and distinct personalities. I decided to start with the female since she was the more docile of the two. We used the same strategy we had utilized with a few other animals. I would stand off to the side and let the caretaker distract her. Then I would approach the cage and as she came to investigate me, I would snap off several shots.

I framed in her face and focused in on the black stripes that defined her orange and white patches. This feline's pink and black nose twitched as she surveyed me. She was quite co-operative and allowed us to do this again and again until I was sure I had a variety of good pictures.

Watching from off to one side, Jay saw how we had used this same technique during the course of the day. The male tiger, a Siberian, was intently watching us as well.

Jay carried my old camera with a smaller lens. He would occasionally snap a photo or two of an animal or of me taking a picture. He decided that since it didn't look that hard, he would get a photograph of the male tiger. He quietly approached the enclosure and placed the lens of his camera on the fencing. The lens was small enough that when he hit the zoom button it protruded into the tiger's cage. Leaning on the fencing, Jay tried to focus, but all he saw through the lens was a blur of bright orange and black. As he moved his head to the side to see why the camera wasn't focusing, the male tiger was charging toward him at a full sprint. His massive feet moved swiftly towards Jay as he opened his mouth and let out a deafening roar.

The sound startled both the caretaker and me. It took a moment to realize what had happened.

We quickly ran toward the far side of the Bengal tiger's cage. My heart was pounding as I ran scanning the area for any signs of Jay. The tiger was still standing on his hind legs with his front paws on the fencing. I wasn't able to see Jay until I rounded the corner of the enclosure.

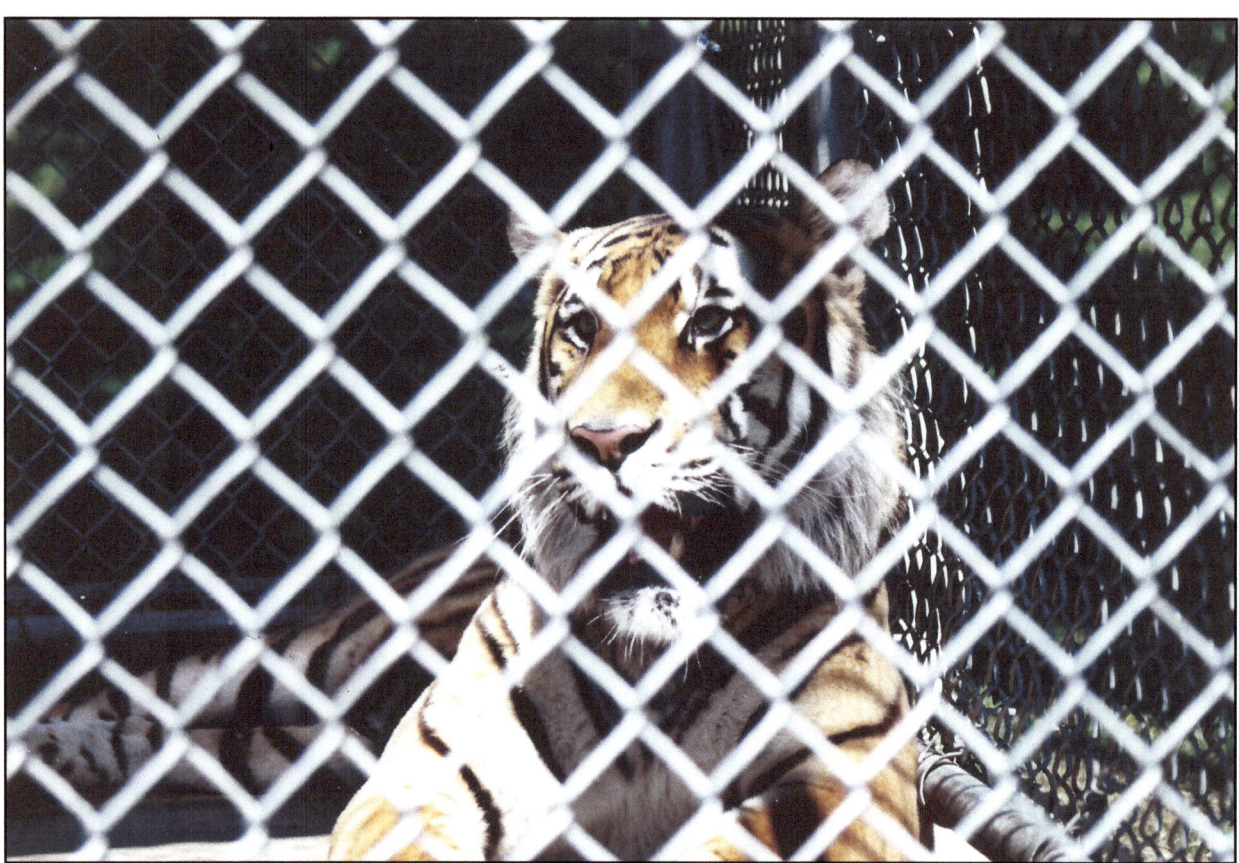

Both the tiger and Jay remained motionless, staring at one another. Luckily, Jay had taken a step backward just as the tiger pounced; avoiding both his large powerful fangs and his razor sharp claws.

Chuckling, the caretaker explained that the male tiger was only a year and a half old and still quite playful.

Jay was shaken, but unharmed. As we walked along the rugged path that led between the animal enclosures toward the truck, Jay swore he had aged ten years in ten seconds.

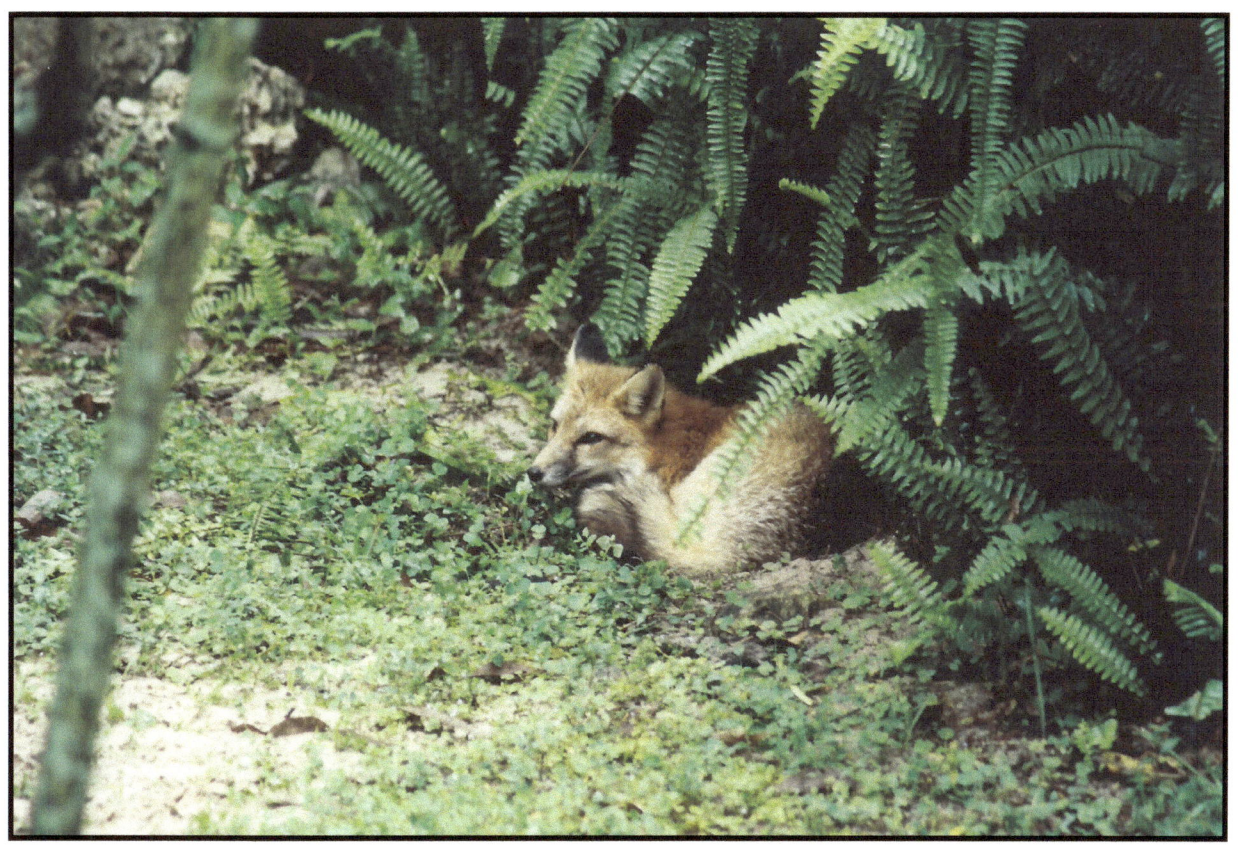

NATIONALLY INTERESTING

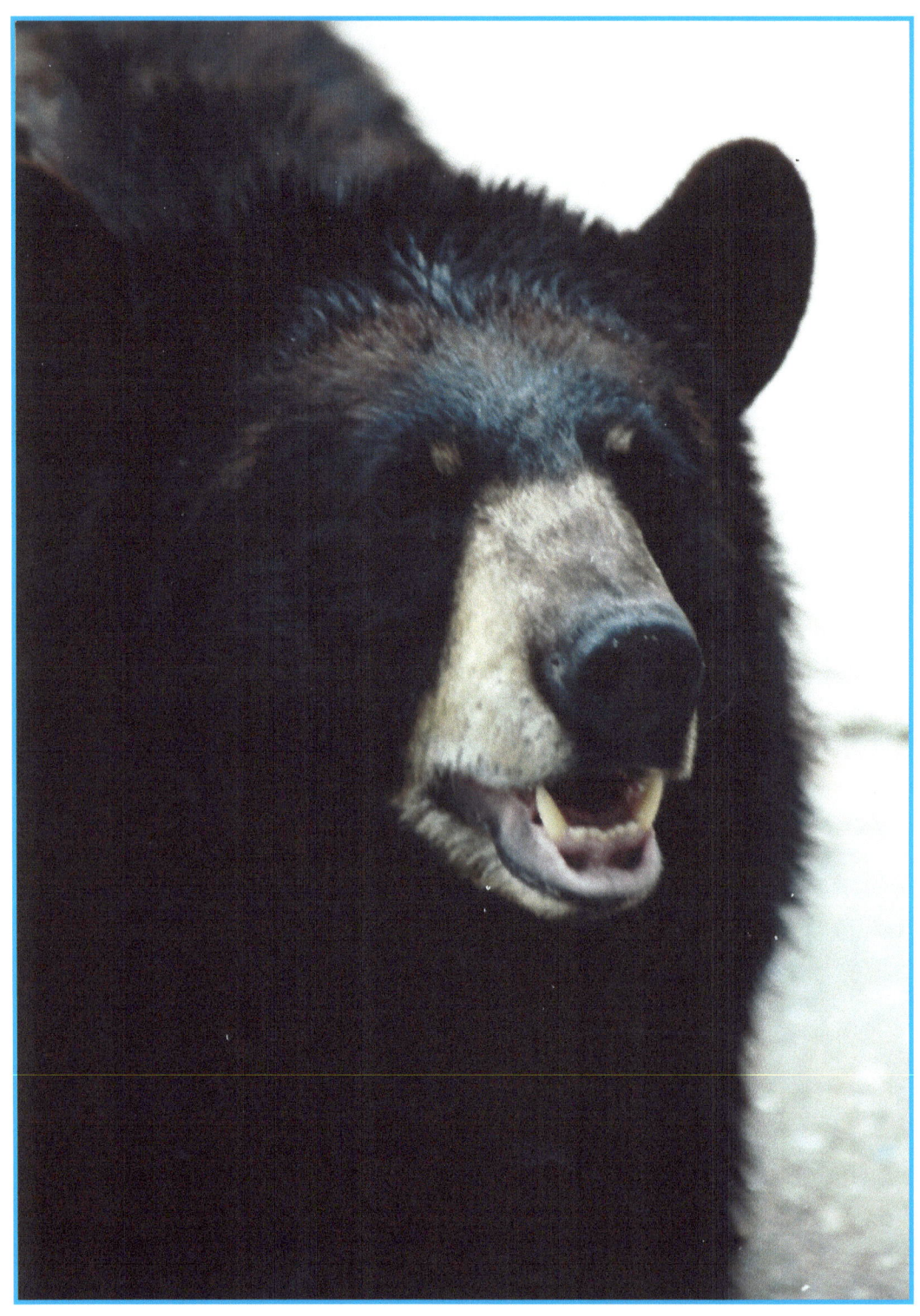

Jay and I arrived at the entrance to the National Park right around sunrise. We followed the road as it wound its way through the woods. At the edge of a scenic overlook, we paused for a few minutes to enjoy the view.

The bright orange sky illuminated the tops of the surrounding mountains. It was early fall and the woods were an array of yellow, orange and red leaves. The shrill calls of a Blue Jay could be heard from somewhere off in the distance.

A brisk autumn wind tapped at the lens as I zoomed in on a lone doe. The colorful leaves surrounded her head like a wreath when she glanced in my direction. Subtle looking tan fur covered most of her body. Her small tail flicked from side to side as I framed her image in the lens. Click.

"Thank You."

Smiling, Jay stood off to my side and pointed across the road. There on a ledge was a juvenile black bear. His fuzzy, pitch-black fur made him look like a giant stuffed animal.

Excited, I quickly clicked off a few shots. Then, quietly I climbed into the back of the truck. Being higher up would get me closer to the bear without disturbing him.

He was busy eating, Click, click went the camera as I focused in on him. With one of his massive claws, he pawed at the ground and snorted. He glanced up momentarily, but seemed unconcerned with my presence, so I tried to get a little closer. Back on the ground, I took a step toward the bear, and then another before taking the shot. I waited for a few moments.

My heart pounding with excitement, I took a single step in his direction. That was one step too many. He ran deep into the woods.

Up the road a small distance, we approached a picnic area. Jay spotted movement near one of the tables. We were both surprised to see several female deer wandering around.

I was able to walk within a few feet of one of the does. Her ears twitched while she dined on the tender grasses. I took a moment to turn the camera and get a vertical shot of her before stepping back and framing in the entire group.

Then I noticed Jay pointing behind me. I turned around to find an enormous male deer standing in a clump of trees.

"Hello. My! You are a big boy. Can you turn your head for me just a little? "

After a moment the buck slowly turned his head, and looked right into the lens. I stood transfixed as we stared at each other.

His large antlers curved upward above his head, topped off by ten distinct points. The front of his thick, strong neck was covered with white fur. Standing straight and proud, he glared at me.

I was between him and the does and he wasn't happy about it.

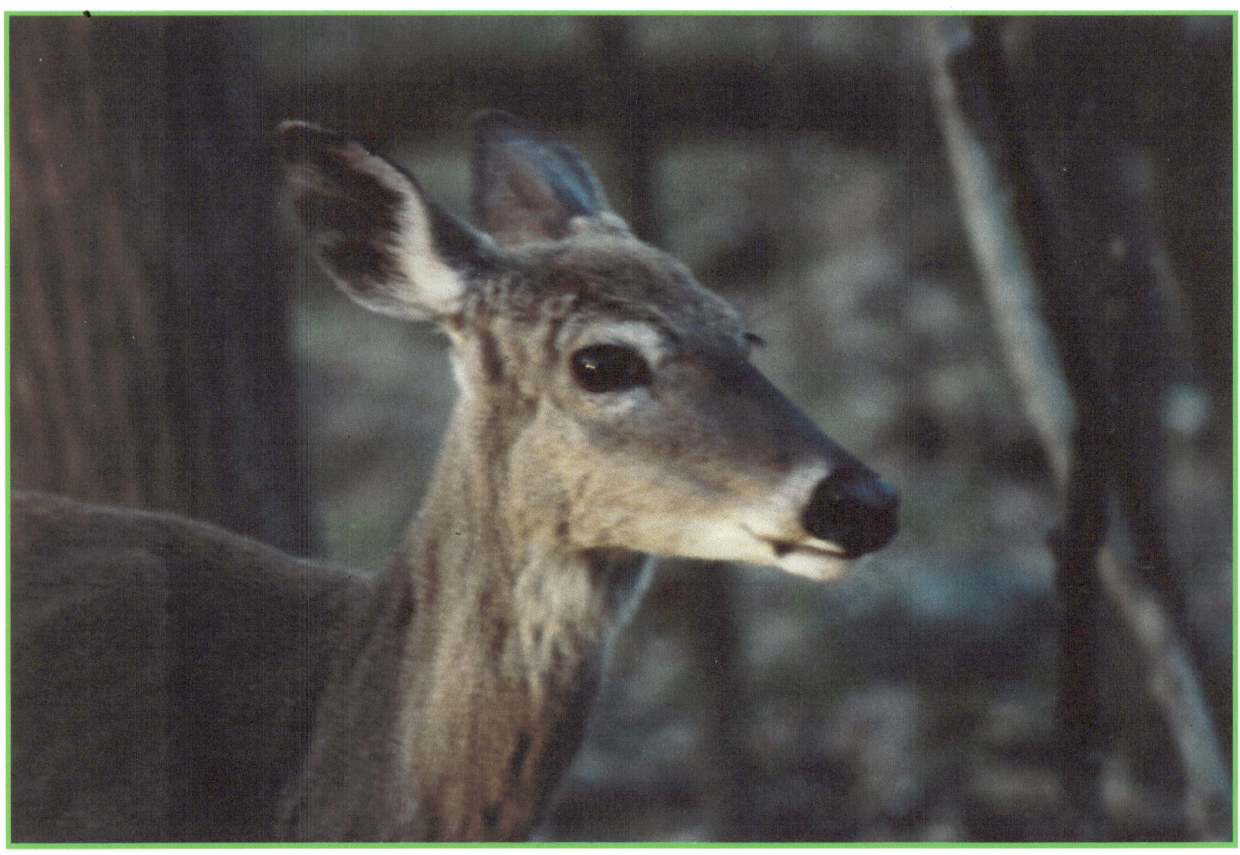

The massive buck stomped his hoof on the ground as I depressed the shutter button. He stomped his hoof again, then snorted at me before lowering his head and pointing his sharp antlers in my direction. This was his way of warning me to leave before he charged.

"Okay, okay, I'm going. "

Depressing the shutter button, I clicked off two more frames while backing away from him. He clearly wasn't in the mood to have his picture taken.

A mile or so up the road Jay saw movement among the trees. We stopped the truck and we both studied the area while trying to determine just what was there.

I got out to investigate. As quietly as I could, I opened the door and slowly slid out of the truck. Crouching down, I used the truck to obscure the animal's view of me.

Stepping around the side of the truck I saw an owl perched among the leaves. Mesmerized by his bright yellow eyes, I stood frozen on the side of road for a moment.

"Hello, Don't worry I won't hurt you. I just want to take your picture."

Nervously, the owl adjusted his grip on the branch. Just as I focused the camera, he spread his wings, covered in feathers of various shades of brown. Click went the camera, just in time to capture a blurry image of the white patch on his chest. I was close enough I could hear the flap of his wings as he departed. I watched as he glided out of sight.

By mid-morning we had only covered a small portion of the park. Little by little, we were encountering more people, so we decided it was time to head home.

Unlike some of our photo trips, this one had been quite successful. I knew the owl and the raccoon had eluded the lens, but I was sure I had some nice photographs of the deer and the bear.

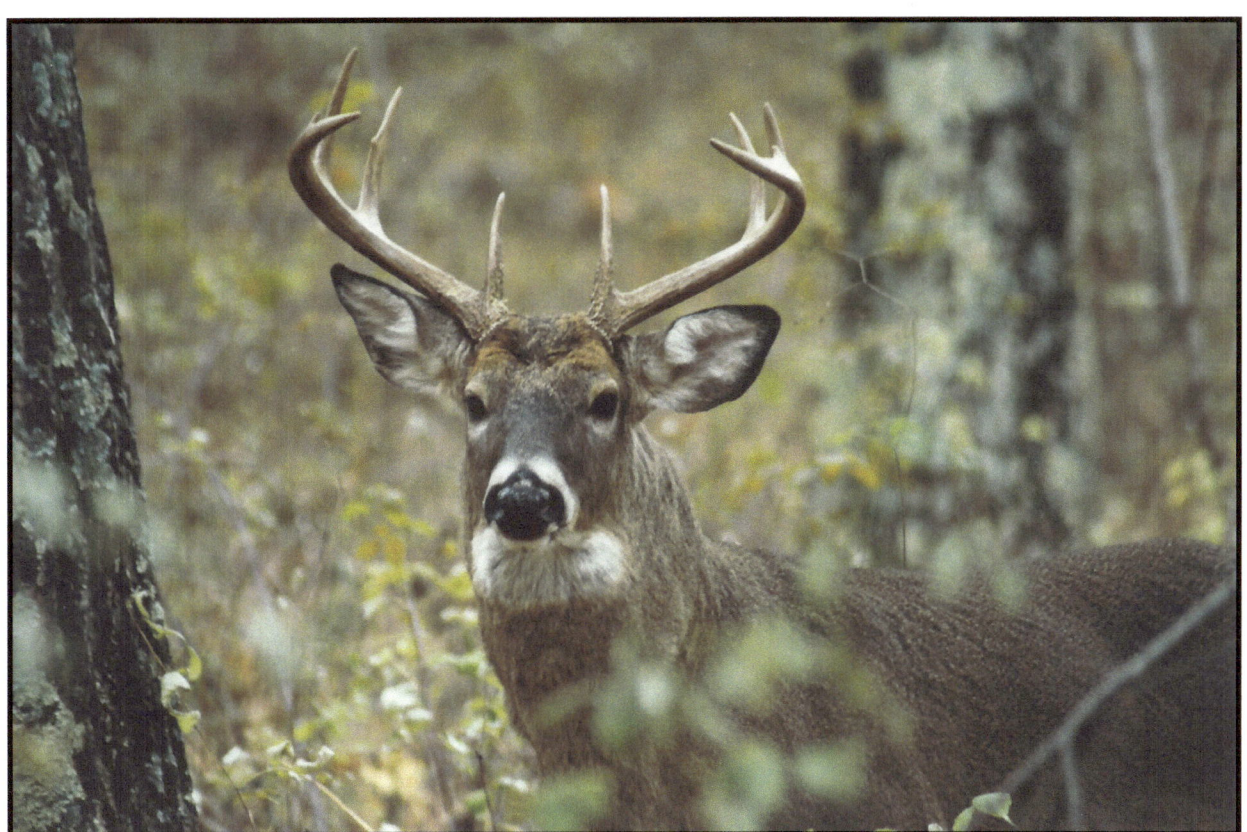

Hoofing It

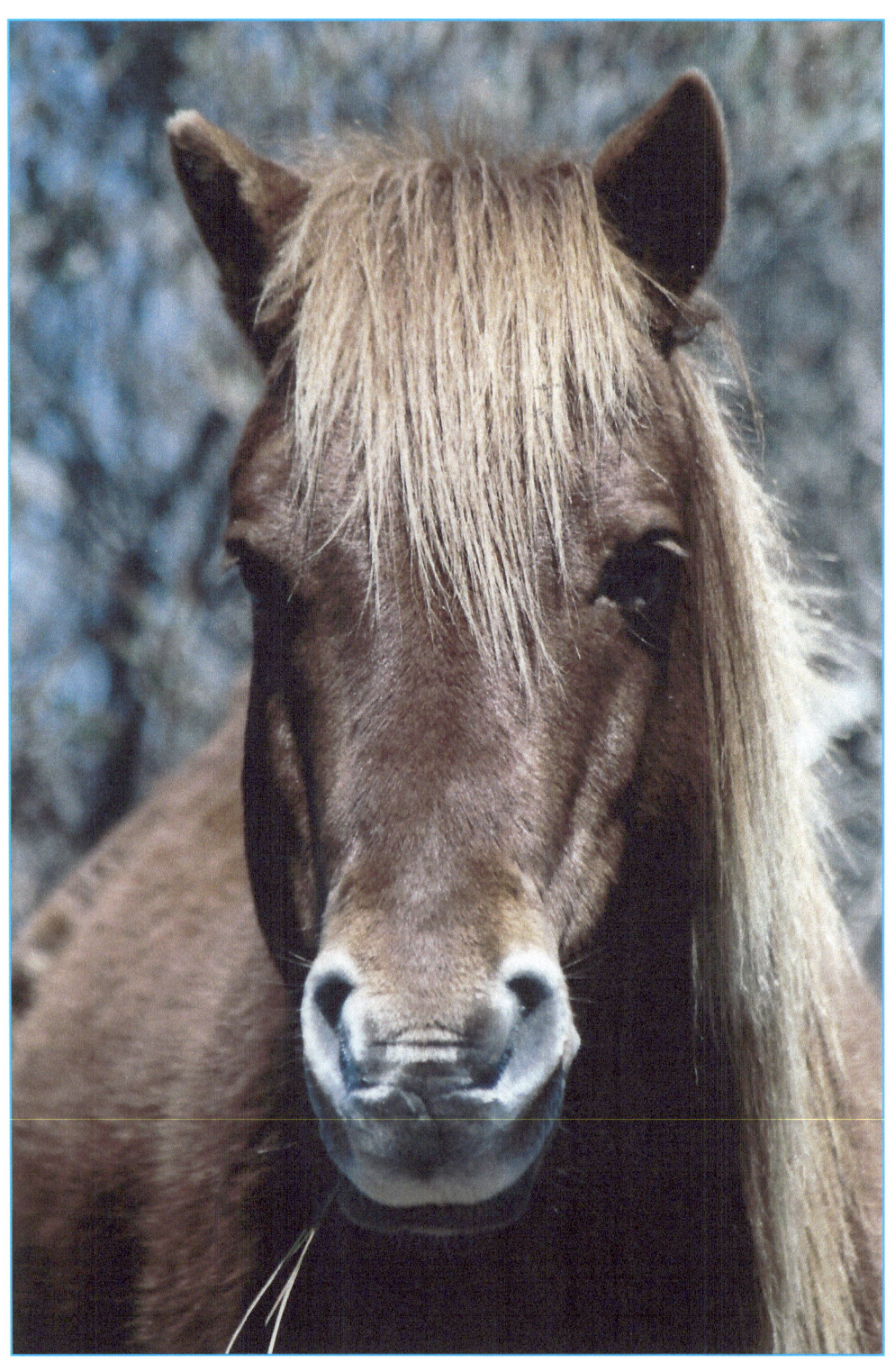

The parking lot was a sea of horse trailers, pick-up trucks and good ole boys in ten-gallon hats. It was five in the morning, and it looked like we had just walked onto the set of a western movie. Strong black coffee seemed to be the beverage of choice, and we were slapped by the aroma when we exited the car. After a short, friendly conversation, we were directed to the man in charge of the "Salt Water Cowboys."

Jake was a rather large man with a muscular build. He stood sipping coffee in his well-worn cowboy boots, faded jeans, and an old denim shirt. Strands of white hair peaked out from beneath his hat. He had a quick smile and listened attentively while I explained my request.

Jake paused for a moment before informing us we wouldn't be able to drive our car to where we needed to be. If we wanted to photograph the wild ponies when they were brought to the corral area, Jay and I would have to walk. Jake grinned when he mentioned it was five miles from the road to the corral. We promised to stay out of harm's way and were given instructions on how to find the trail that led to our destination.

It was past dawn when Jay located the trail-head and we ventured out into the woods. Under cloudy skies, we wandered down the narrow path and chatted about nothing in particular. The sound of our voices carried in the chilly morning air and, along with the sound of our footsteps, broke the silence. A gentle autumn breeze played with the leaves on the trees so large that they seemed to go on forever.

"So do you think it really is five miles or do you think he just didn't want us out there in the way?" I asked.

Jay glanced at me and smiled. "I think we're going to find out. "

After walking for what seemed like an eternity we came to a clearing. There we found a small group of people hanging out in the middle of nowhere. They were friends and relatives of the Salt Water Cowboys. The last report they had was that the boys had located most of the herd and were heading them our way. They were a few miles off along the beach, so it would be a while before they arrived.

Hunger pains tapped at my stomach as raindrops began to fall. We had crackers, peanuts, cupcakes, water, and soda in the car—five miles away. It was now well past noon and we hadn't stopped for breakfast. Jay pulled a miniature candy bar out of his pocket and offered me half.

"Umm, lunch".

Just as I was savoring the last bit of chocolate, we could hear something off in the distance. Suddenly, up over the hill, we spotted a small group of ponies running wildly toward us.

"Heads up! Here they come!" someone shouted. I reached for my camera and before I knew it the sound of thunder engulfed me.

Jay and I took shelter behind an old pickup truck. As the herd approached, a huge black stallion announced his displeasure at the situation. His wild eyes surveyed me as the ponies plowed past us, through the opening in the fence and into the corral. Quickly, an older gentleman closed the gate behind them.

It seemed like only seconds later that another group of ponies, being coaxed on by a few cowboys on horseback, came galloping into the clearing. This group wasn't quite as willing to enter the corral. They ran toward it full force, and then suddenly turned. With the cowboys behind them, they had no place to go.

Hoofing It

I clicked off frame after frame while the panicked ponies searched for an escape route. I focused in on one member of the group. Her worn white coat showed her age. The old girl's matted mane hung loosely over her thin neck. Her sorrowful eyes hinted at the hard life she had led. The long hot summer had not been good to her. Although she paced from side to side, she didn't seem as distressed as the other members of her group.

The cowboys waved their hats to urge the ponies toward the corral. One of the ponies began snorting and stomping his feet, while another circled nervously. Suddenly the black stallion in the corral reared up, kicking his feet wildly and snorting back at the painted pony in the clearing.

Then, over the hill, came another large group of ponies being chased by more cowboys on horseback. Before they knew it, this small stubborn herd was swallowed up into the larger one and shuffled into the corral.

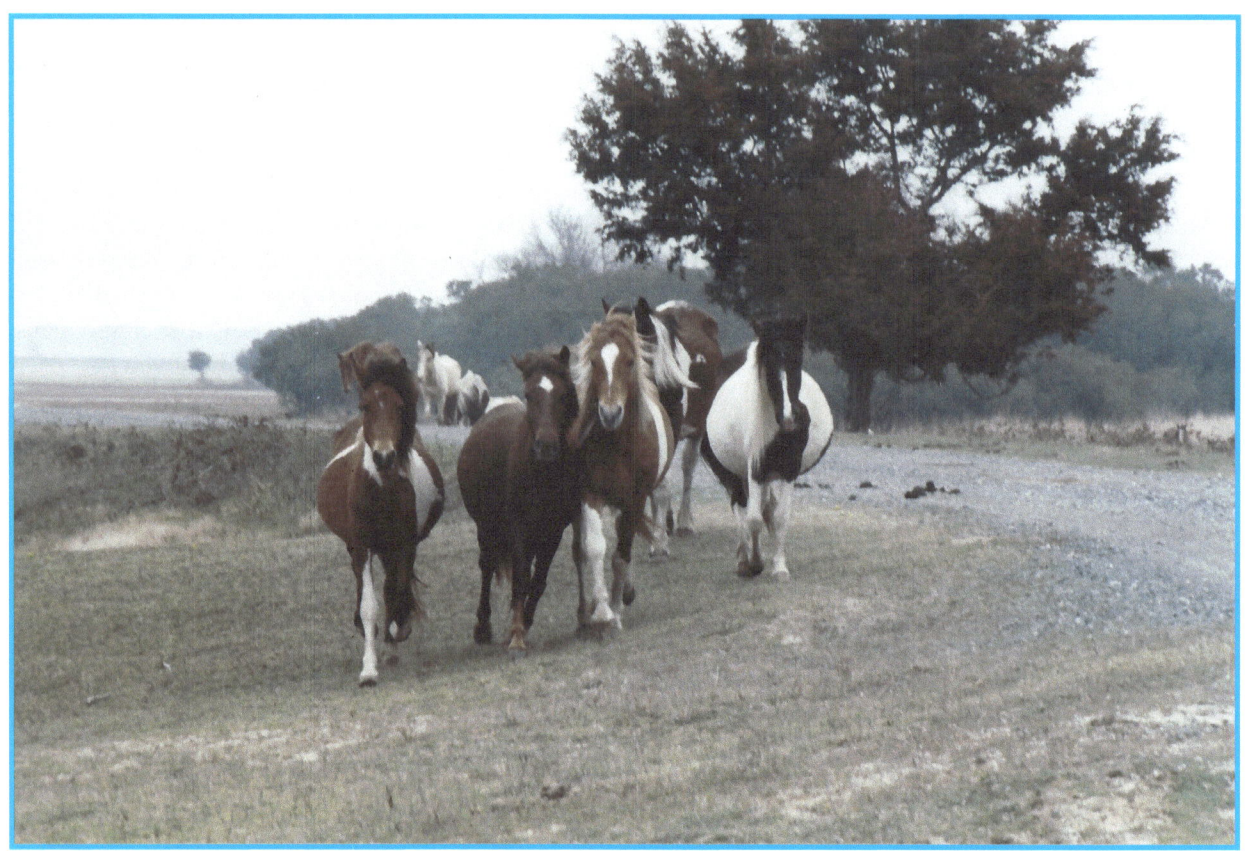

As the old wooden gate slammed shut, a celebratory yell echoed in the autumn air.

"HEE HAW, we got 'em boys."

One by one the ponies began to settle down, and I approached the corral. The old timer that had manned the gate glanced over at me with a concerned look on his face. I held up my camera.

"Telephoto lens, I'm not getting anywhere near them, I promise," I shouted.

His weathered face softened and I caught a glimpse of a smile.

Amongst the sea of legs there was one lone colt being jolted from side to side by the larger ponies. He wiggled and pushed and eventually made his way to the fence.

"Hello, Sweetie, mind if I take your picture?"

His soft chestnut colored body was held up on four white spindly legs. I zoomed in on his long dark nose and focused on the white patch between his eyes. His ears twitched when Mom whinnied for him. He shook his head, tossing his long mane from side to side, before retreating back into the herd and arriving safely by his mother's side.

It was raining steadily now and I had a nice variety of pictures. Although we were both glad we came, neither of us was looking forward to the long hike back to the car. Jay and I thanked the cowboys for their help, headed into the woods and down the trail. A canopy of leaves sheltered us from the rain. We were tired, hungry, and pretty dirty too. We decided on a quick bite to eat and a long hot shower. Then, we would sit down and pick tomorrow's destination.

After walking for nearly half an hour, we heard a squeaking noise from behind us. When we turned to look, an old faded red pickup truck came around the bend. The truck was covered with a variety of dents and scrapes, and we were both surprised to see the shiny new horse trailer it was pulling. We moved to the side of the trail to let the truck go by, but it stopped. The young driver barely looked fifteen years old. His freckled face lit up when he smiled and he offered us a ride back to our car.

The bumpy ride was filled with chatter about the critters that I had photographed and the locations we had visited. Back at the car, we said our good byes and waved as Bob drove toward home. He planned to relay the day's events to his parents over dinner and tell them that he had met a real wildlife photographer. Before this trip I had never heard of a Salt Water Cowboy. I too now have a story to tell.

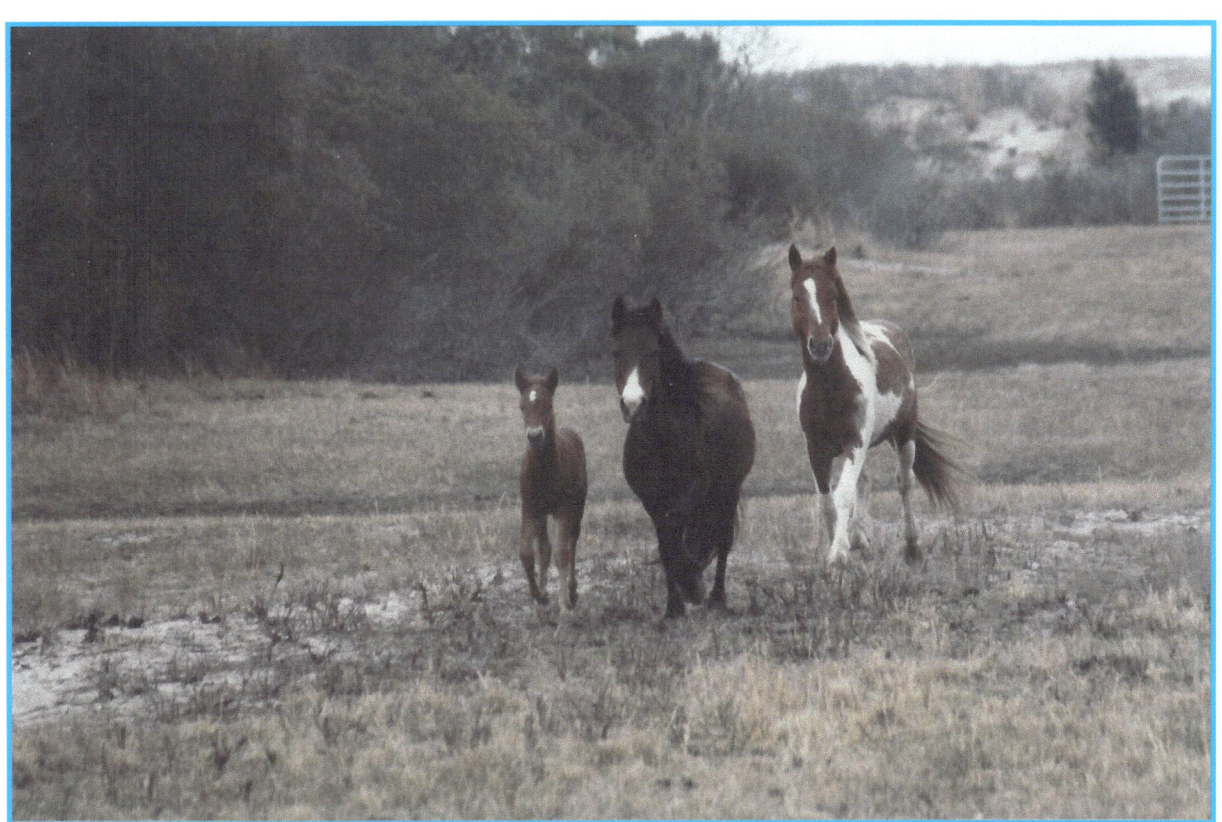

GOT ANY BOBCAT PHOTOGRAPHS?

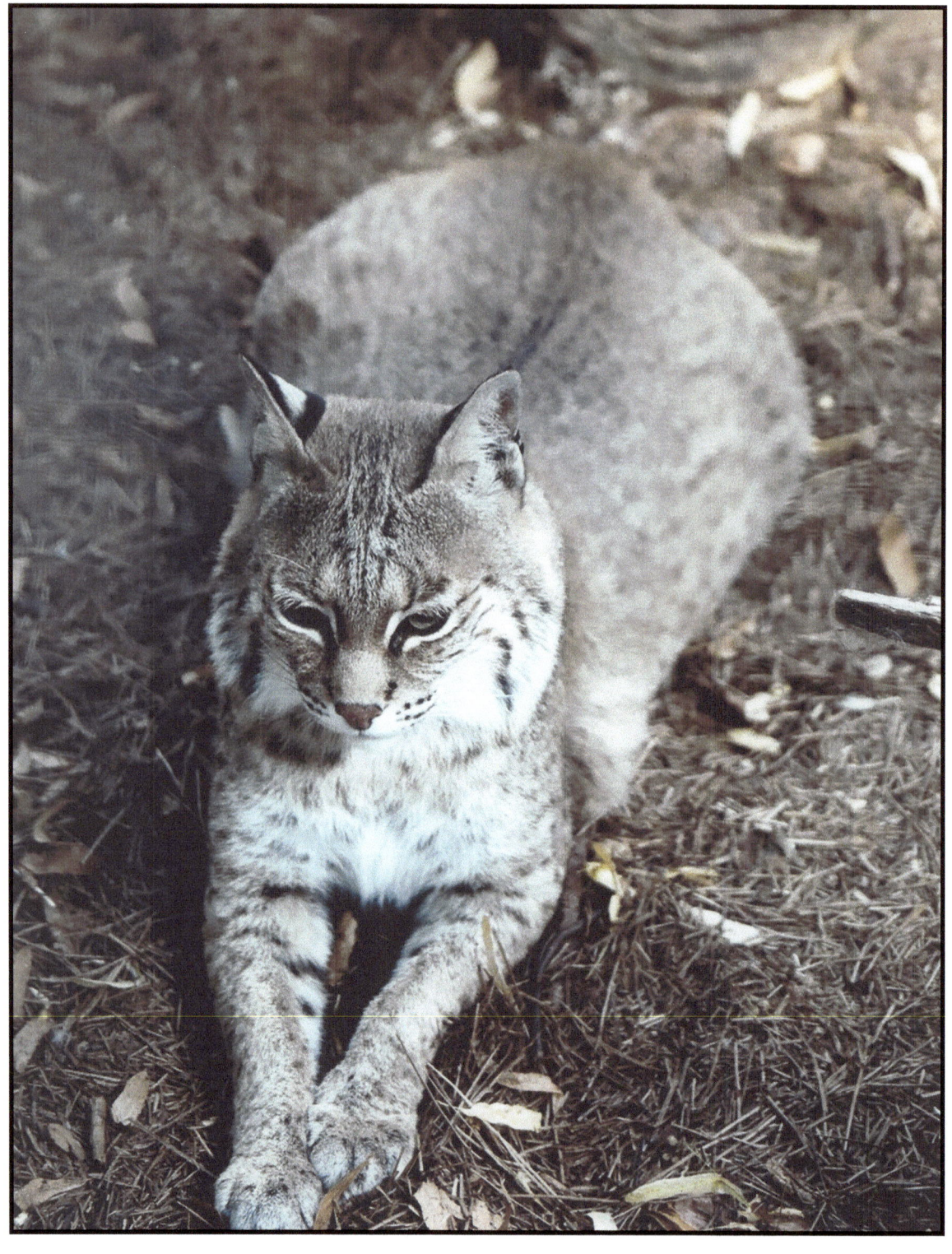

Although I pursue new subjects constantly, I don't always have the image someone is looking for. When this happens, often the conversation moves on to focus on the desired animal. That wasn't the case when a magazine editor contacted me. The conversation moved on to the similarities between a lynx and a bobcat, and then ended with me thanking her for thinking of me.

Silly me, I thought I had lost the sale and the editor would simply move on to another photographer. Less than an hour later the phone rang. It was the same editor, only this time she asked if I could get a bobcat photograph. I couldn't believe what she was asking. We weren't talking about a dog or domestic cat; bobcats are wild animals and quite shy. There was a reason she was having trouble finding the photograph she wanted.

Bright and early the next day, Jay and I were up and on the road. It took a bit of work, but I had located a small zoo that would allow me to come in and take photographs of their bobcats. During the ride, we discussed what we might find when we arrived. The cats could very well be uncooperative: bobcats are nocturnal, and they could be sleeping. Perhaps we wouldn't be able to get close enough to get good photographs; there might be fencing in the way. There were a million things that could go wrong, and I had someone waiting for these shots.

After the long ride, we finally arrived at our destination. We entered through the back gate, and headed for the office. Once there, we were given directions to the bobcat's location and instructed not to get in the enclosure.

While Jay and I walked along the narrow path, we discussed our surprise at being left alone. I fully expected someone to escort us or, at least, discuss these particular cats with us.

The barking sounds of a howler monkey echoed through the air. The mighty roar of a lion startled us when we passed his domain.

Then, there they were. Two bobcats.

As I glanced over at them, all my nervousness disappeared.

"Hello there. Jay, look how beautiful they are."

They were awake and roaming around the enclosure. I captured them on film from a distance to gauge their reaction. Observing me, they sat quietly and didn't seem to mind the flash at all.

Carefully, I stepped over the outside barrier and took another shot. I was able to walk right up to the enclosure, press the lens against the fencing, and capture the close-up shot I needed.

Click, click, went the camera as I focused in again. Then I zoomed in for an even closer shot.

The bobcats speckled coat glistened in the morning sun; subtle dark brown lines ran from the bridge of his nose up his forehead. Black and white stripes began below the tip of his nose and extended to the sides of his face. His long white whiskers accentuated the white fur on his chin.

I stood for a moment just enjoying being this close to them.

Jay and I conversed back and forth, and the cats would turn to look at whoever was talking, as if they were following the conversation. This gave me the opportunity to get some profile shots of each of them.

Got Any Bobcat Photographs?

We moved slowly, careful not to startle them. If I spooked either one of them, they would both run for the safety of their shelter.

I knelt down and peered through the lens. The bobcat looked right at me. Instead of taking the shot, I peered into his eyes and focused in on the black lines that outlined them, and then I pressed the shutter button.

Slowly, I approached the other cat.

"Hello, sweetheart, mind if I take a few pictures of you?"

"Quit talking to them and take pictures," Jay whispered.

As I focused, the other cat walked over and I quickly framed in the pair. Then I managed to zoom in quite close on his face. Through the lens, I could truly count his whiskers. Observing the pair, I wondered what they must have been thinking. One of the cats stood up and stretched.

Click, click, click went the camera as I finished off a roll of film.

Then he turned and showed me the cute little bobbed tail that they were known for.

Four rolls of film later, we returned to the office, thanked them for their help, and made a small donation to the zoo.

By that afternoon, the film was developed; I had picked out several photographs and sent them via special delivery to the magazine. It had been a very enjoyable, accomplished day, which we finished off with a pizza for dinner.

The following afternoon, I received a phone call from the magazine. They thanked me for the photographs, and were quite pleased with my work. However, while I was out taking the pictures, they found someone else who already had them, and they had purchased his instead. I ended the conversation by thanking them for thinking of me and encouraged her contact me again.

Although I was disappointed, I was reminded of a valuable lesson I had learned early in my photography career. In the publishing world, no matter how good your work is, you have to have what a publisher wants, in their hands, just when they want it, to make the sale.

The next time a publisher wanted bobcat photographs, I had them. I knew that our experience with the bobcats was worth all the trouble.

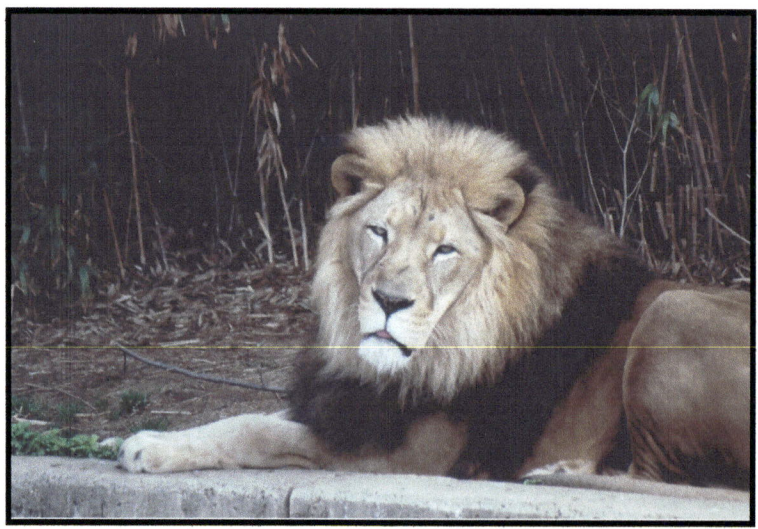

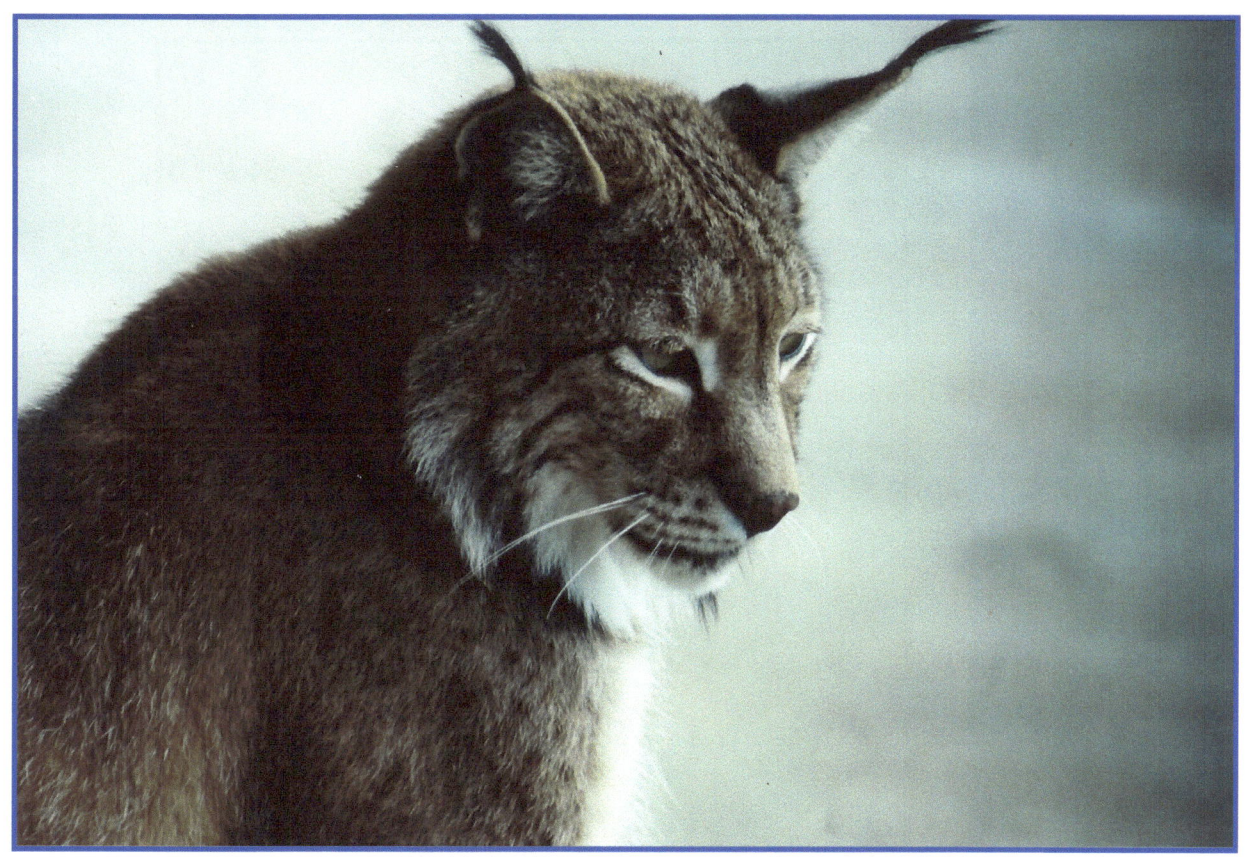

PREHISTORIC ENCOUNTERS

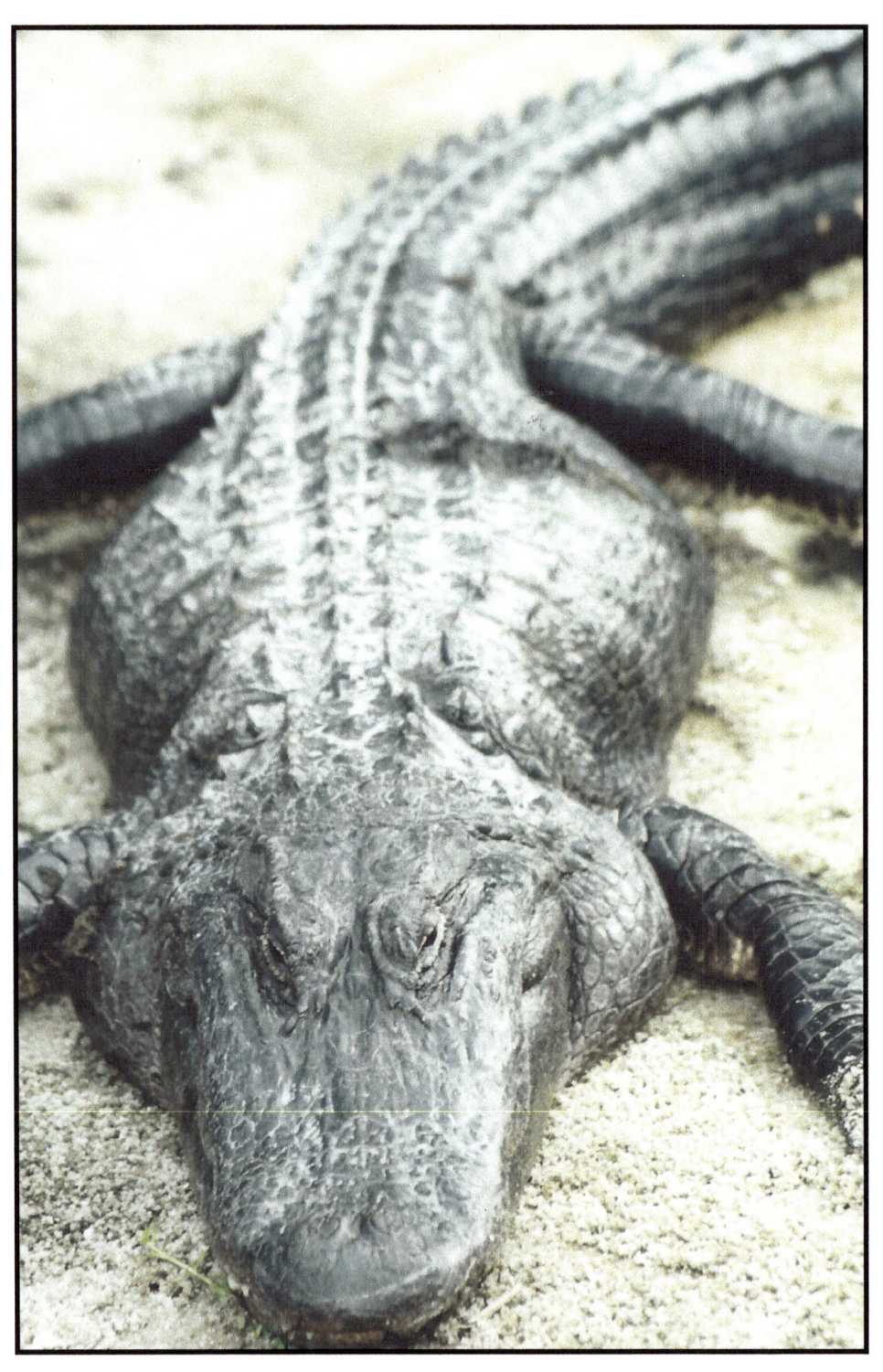

Jay and I left our motel room in the predawn hours. We headed toward the swamps for which this area of Georgia was famous. Discovering a rough dirt path wide enough to drive down, we left civilization behind. As the truck twisted and turned, I studied the landscape. But we were just a little too early. There was barely enough light to see anything.

Along the sides of the dirt road were small canals filled with water, perfect places to spot alligators.

Jay drank a cup of coffee when we stopped and waited for the sun to rise. Meanwhile, I spent the time organizing my camera lens and film while munching on crackers.

As sunlight began to dance in the tall marsh grasses, we resumed our quest and discovered another pond. On the far side of the pond, Jay saw movement just beyond a clump of tall grass. The area was totally still; no breeze, no birds singing, no movement, no sounds.

Then, what looked like a branch floating in the water came into view. Through the camera lens, I wasn't sure what it was. But, after a few minutes, I began to think Jay was right.

It could be an alligator.

Sitting quietly at the edge of the water for over an hour, we watched the form slowly float closer.

Dark gray clouds drifted across the sky as large raindrops penetrated the water's surface.

I was able to focus in and clearly saw it was indeed an alligator. He wasn't as large as I had expected and was barely moving, but was definitely an alligator.

"Smile," I whispered.

The alligator eventually made his way to my side of the pond.

Through the lens, he looked right at me with his black menacing eyes. Sunlight broke through and reflected in the camera lens, obscuring my view. Carefully repositioning myself, I was able to observe him from another angle.

His rough leathery face gave him an intimidating look.

On my stomach at the water's edge, I nervously clicked the shutter as he drifted closer and closer. Jay returned from getting my jacket, and quietly encouraged me to move away from the water's edge. He was right; I needed to back away so that I could enjoy more alligator encounters in the future.

As we drove away, there was another alligator in one of the canals. After stopping the truck, I exited and edged closer to the water.

Focusing my camera, I noticed a baby alligator as well. This was dangerous; Mom could see me as a threat. Taking a few steps back, I knelt down to take the shot.

The marsh grass that concealed the baby swayed in the breeze. I framed in the mother alligator's long snout that filled the lens. With a swift wave of her front leg, she let me know she didn't welcome my presence.

"Okay, I'm outta here."

It would be a few days before I finally encountered my first huge alligator. Jay and I had been out on a boat ride looking for more subjects. Heading back to shore, we discussed our options. Then, Jay spotted the largest alligator we had ever seen. There he was, stretched out on the bank in the midday sun. His large body compressed the sand as he slumbered.

"Oh wow! I have to get a picture of him!"

In a flash, I was out of the boat making my way across the sand. Clicking the shutter from a distance, I moved closer. Kneeling to get a better angle, it was obvious this guy was massive. I marveled at his size and the thick jagged scales that ran down his back and tail. I clicked off another frame, and then crawled closer, lying on the ground in front of him. Then his ominous eyes opened and he glared at me.

I had come too close to him; I could actually hear his breathing. My trembling finger stayed on the shutter and the camera clicked continuously while my mind raced. What were the warning signs alligators gave? Their striking distance was how far? This is how wildlife photographers get themselves into trouble. I had been so engrossed in my subject that I forgot about the danger.

The alligator could easily grab me with his powerful jaws in an instant. His claws were huge and could shred my limbs with very little effort. He seemed quite calm, not the least bit upset by my presence, but able to strike in an instant. I backed off slowly and carefully. It was very important not to startle him. This was a dangerous position to be in and I wanted to get out of it in one piece.

"I'm going to back away and let you go back to sleep,". I informed him. "See, I'm leaving you alone."

I never took my eyes off of that alligator; if he came at me, I wanted a chance to evade him. Crawling ever so slowly backward, I was thankful for each growing inch of distance between us. His menacing eyes watched my every move.

Then something grabbed the back of my sweatshirt! I had been so focused on putting space between that alligator and me, I had no idea what was behind me. With a quick jolt I was propelled backwards.

Thankfully, I was a safe distance from the threat in front of me, but, what was behind me? Panicked, I looked over my shoulder and realized it was Jay dragging me away from the alligator. With a sigh of relief, I stood up. As we walked away, Jay scolded me and scowled while reminding me that I could have been lunch.

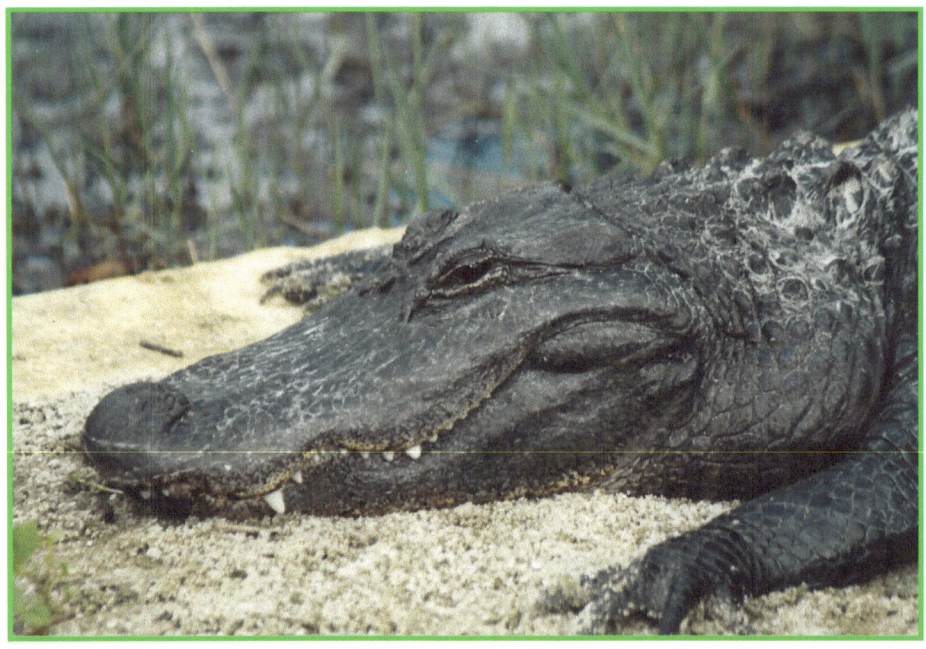

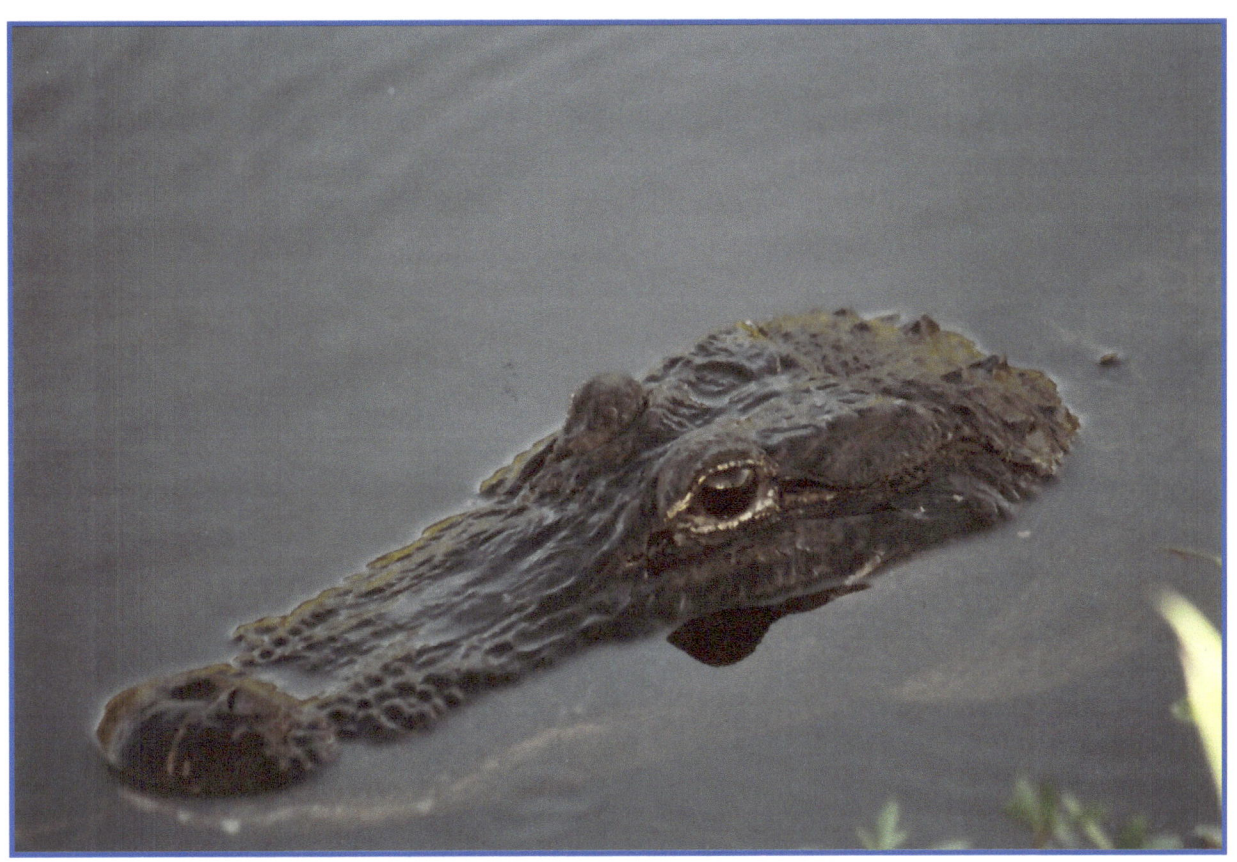

Snowy Adventures

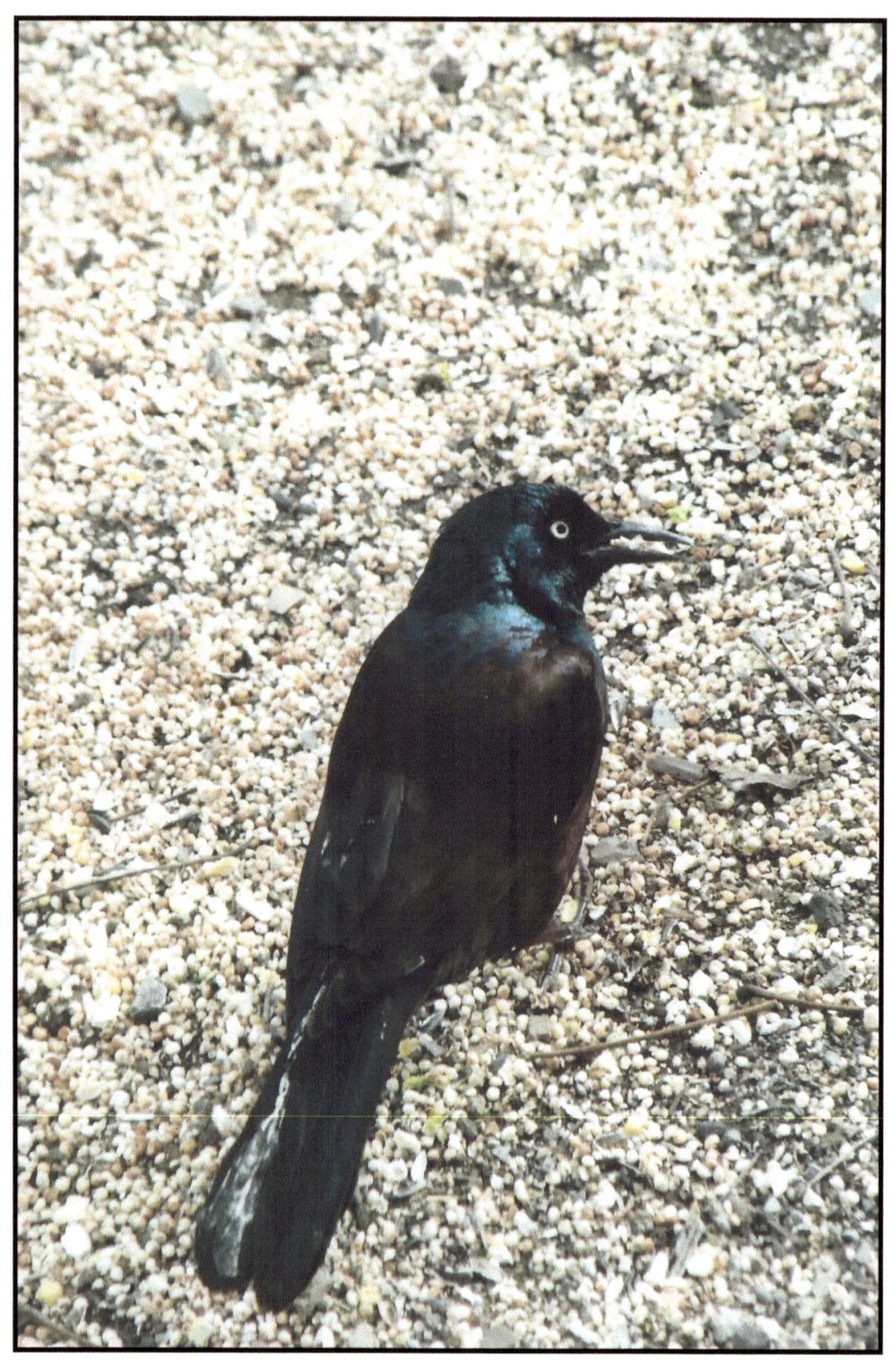

I t had been a long, snowy winter and I was really ready for spring. I started each day by filling the bird feeders and chopping ice out of the birdbaths. I then picked a location and sat to see what feathered friends would show up. I dressed in layers and wore two thin pairs of gloves so my hands wouldn't shake.

Taking pictures in the snow proved to be a new challenge. The stark white background often affected the images, so my first winter pictures didn't quite turn out as expected.

After a few rolls of film, and some adjustments, I was getting some beautiful shots of birds in the snow. Peering through the lens at these delicate creatures, I wondered why they had chosen to stay here in the bitter cold.

Each picture taking session was finished off with a warm cup of tea and a sense of accomplishment.

Slowly winter released its grip, and the icy world around me began to melt, a little. The temperatures warmed up enough to coax me out to the woods to look for new subjects to photograph.

To the casual observer, Jay and I were an average couple out for a ride on a sunny day. Our truck followed a line of traffic that was slowly winding its way along the mountain road. Most of the other drivers were probably wishing that traffic would move faster, but not us. We were intently watching the surrounding woods and skies for any sign of movement.

We traveled across a familiar bridge where we had spotted wildlife before. We knew that vultures, herons, ducks, geese, and even Bald Eagles frequented the area.

Glancing at the rocks and water below, my heart jumped with excitement. There was something in the river below us.

"Is that what I think it is?" I shouted.

"It sure looked like it to me." Jay responded.

Impatiently, Jay drove the rest of the way across the bridge. Within seconds, we were skidding to a stop on the side of the road. I quickly jumped out, with my camera in hand.

Proceeding across the road, I waved to the driver behind us. "Sorry, thanks for not running me over."

Stepping over the guardrail, I descended the incline. In my excitement, I hadn't noticed how steep the hillside was, or the depth of the snow in this area. There was a lot of brush to maneuver through; the snow was over my knees.

At the bottom, I thought there was a Bald Eagle perched on a stump. Hopefully, he would remain totally engrossed in gorging himself on a fish and not fly off to quickly.

Each step took an enormous effort, and my progress was very slow. I decided to sit and slide down the embankment. Banging into a few trees and sliding into bushes, I made my way to the bottom. The river was beyond the next clump of trees. I stumbled as I climbed over a down tree. Then took a moment to compose myself and try to harness my excitement. I wasn't to the river yet, and I was soaking wet and covered with snow. After brushing some of the snow off, I emerged from the group of trees. Inching my way toward the river, I carefully scanned the area for any signs of the Bald Eagle.

Snowy Adventures

Through the lens, I searched for the familiar white feathers of an eagles head and tail. The sounds of the rushing water filled the air as it cascaded over the rocks that were dispersed between the river banks.

Then something moved in the water in front of me. As my eyes focused on the movement, my heart sank. It wasn't an eagle after all, it wasn't even a bird. It was a fisherman dressed in dark brown clothes with a white hat on. Stepping out from the tree line, I startled him as he was casting his line. Disappointed, I turned and walked along the bank, hoping for an easier route back to the road.

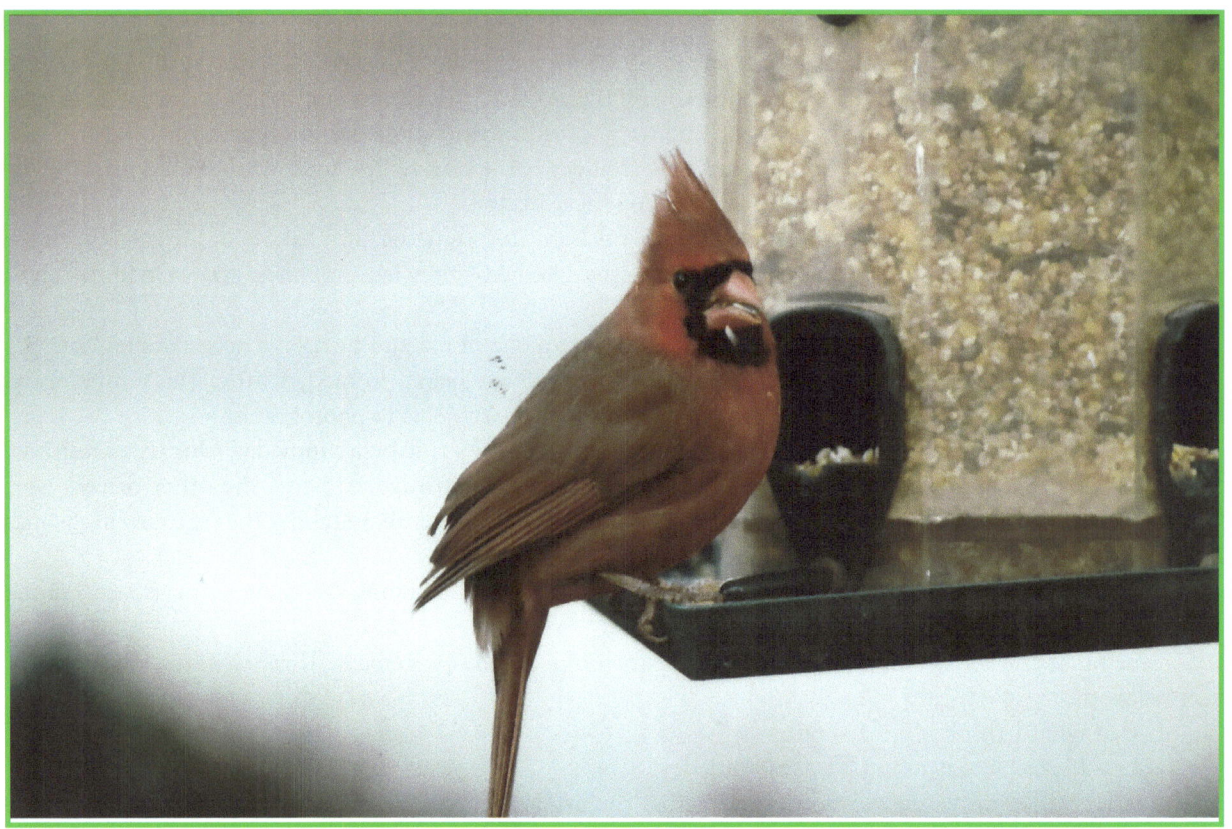

Downriver, I spied three does. They had selected an area in the sunshine. The warm sun had slowly melted the snow, and fresh green sprouts were beginning to emerge. Glancing up for a moment, they posed for me.

I soon found a narrow trail that wound its way up through the woods at a steady incline. There weren't going to be any new Bald Eagle images today, but I did get a bit of exercise.

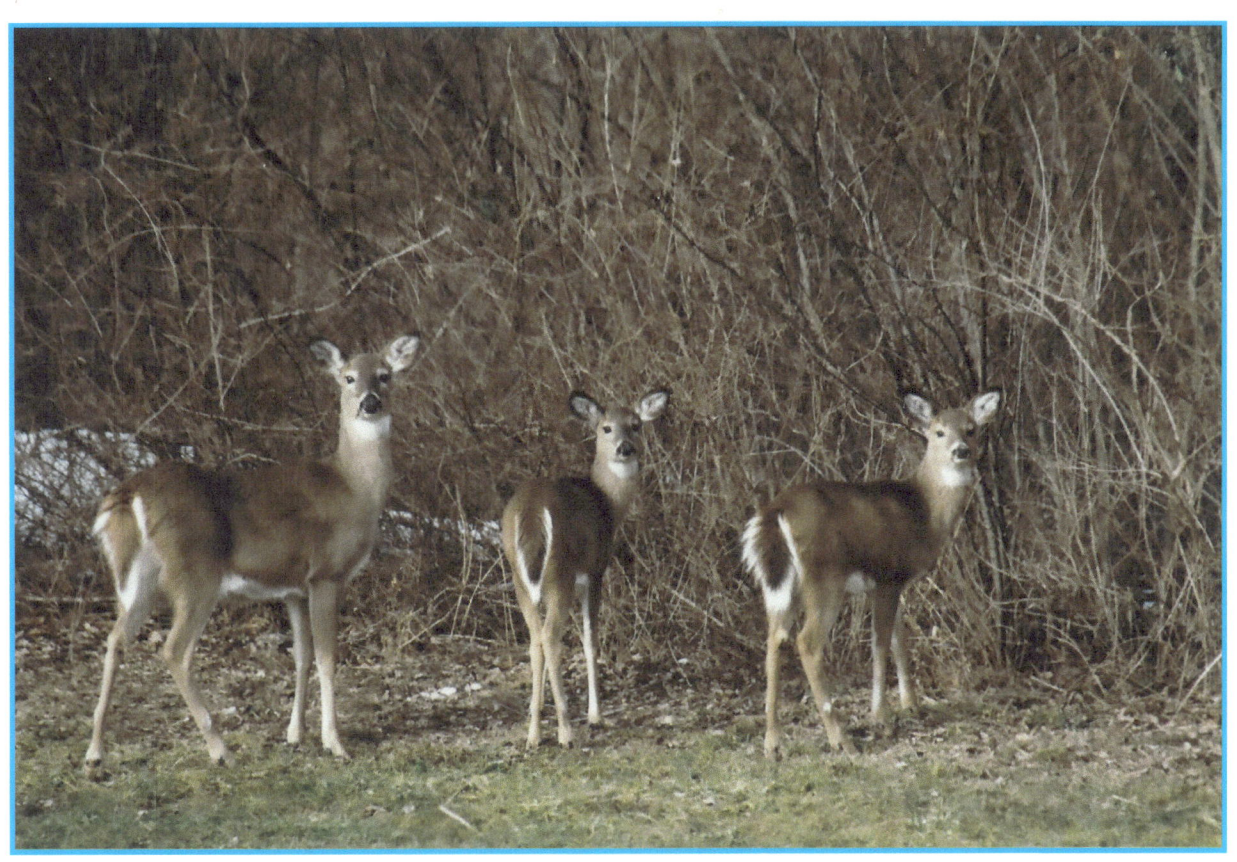

BEARLY RED

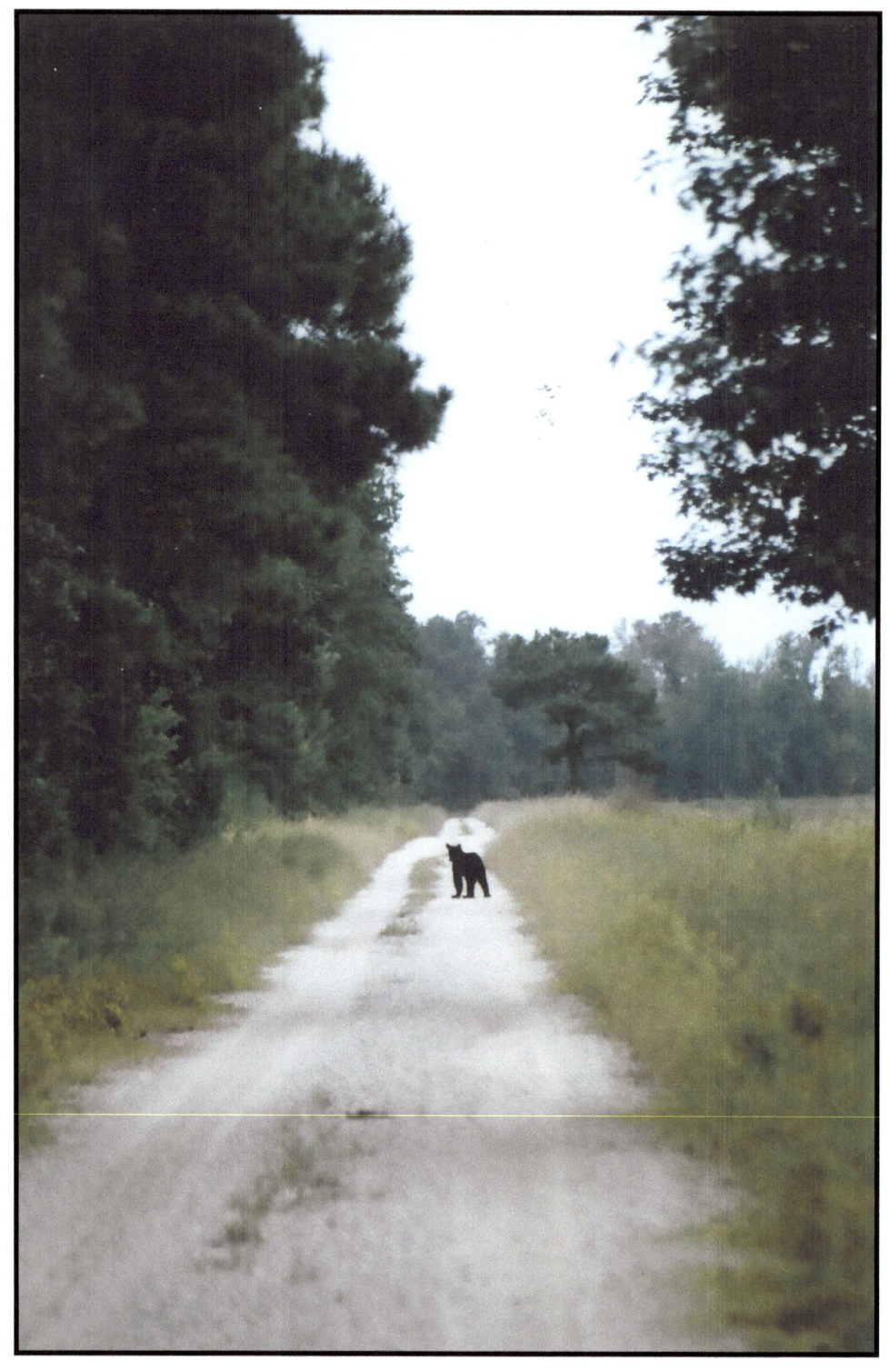

There were two types of animals on my wish list for our trip to North Carolina: Black Bears and Red Wolves. Since this area of the state had the largest concentration of Black Bears in the Eastern United States, Black Bears would hopefully be easy to find. Finding one of the very small number of Red Wolves would be a bit tougher. Red Wolves by nature are quite shy and generally avoid people, but we had several days and there was always the possibility of a chance encounter.

We entered the refuge at dawn. A small dust cloud followed us while we made our way along the rough road. The refuge consisted of a series of fields and wooded areas that were landscaped to be animal friendly. Canals filled with water lined the roadways. A dark form moved across the open field to our left minutes after we arrived. By the time I was sure it was a Black Bear, it was nearly to the tree line. This bear was rather shy and I wouldn't be getting any pictures of him today.

Several hundred yards up the road, near the edge of a corn field, was a more curious Black Bear. Standing on his hind legs, he peaked out from between the stalks to observe us. From the safety of the truck, I took a few shots. Then, from beside the truck, I took a few more.

Slowly, I stepped into the roadway and knelt down. Black fur filled the frame when the camera focused in on his tan snout.

"Click, click," went the camera, finishing off another roll of film.

My fumbling in my pocket for more film made him nervous. Slowly, he began to walk away.

Since he was strolling along, and not in any real hurry, I followed him. Pausing to get the bear in frame, I clicked off several more shots.

He was steadily increasing his pace to put more distance between us. I took this as my cue to head back to the truck. His pace increased and by the time he reached the wood line he quickly vanished into the underbrush.

Just before sunset, we drove through a wooded area. Jay spotted a bear in the truck's rear view mirror. My excitement grew as we reversed our way back to the bear. Perhaps this one would let me get a little closer. There really wasn't enough light for a larger lens, but I wanted to try it anyway.

The black form stood motionless in the center of the road. It was a juvenile, and he probably wasn't sure if we were a threat or not. While he decided what to do, he began swaying from side to side. This nervous motion made it difficult to focus in on him.

"Come on, sweetie, hold still for just a second," I whispered.

After playing with shutter speed, focus, and angles, I put the lens of the camera through the open back window of the truck and captured him on film. A sudden gust of wind rustled the branches of the trees; this prompted the bear to run for the safety of a nearby canal. By the time we were out of the truck, he had disappeared into the water. I had never known that Black Bears were such great swimmers.

Back in the truck we emerged from the woods, and spotted a farmer working on his tractor in the nearby field. The sounds of the diesel engine filled the air. I was sure this would scare off any wildlife in the area. We were just about to move on to another location, when we saw a bear standing on her hind legs looking out over the field. She clearly wasn't concerned with our presence. Then, Jay spotted her baby on the other side of the field.

That was when we realized I was photographing Mom while she searched for her cub, which was on the opposite side of the tractor and clearly afraid. Mom stood up again and looked across the field. I took this opportunity to get a few quick shots of her from a distance. Mom then returned to standing on all four legs and began to pace. Jay and I decided to leave the area so there would be one less obstacle between Mom and baby.

We returned to the refuge in the morning. The smell of the late summer rain from the night before still lingered in the air. Slowly, the truck crept along a dirt path we hadn't explored before. A lone deer stood on an embankment on the opposite side of the canal. Carefully, I framed him in the lens.

"Good morning," I uttered softly.

The buck went back to enjoying his breakfast of clover while I repositioned myself a bit closer. After taking a few more photographs, I moved to the very edge of the canal. Only some murky water and a dozen or so feet stood between me and my subject. By leaning forward, I was able to zoom in on his face and capture him on film.

As I clicked the shutter button, I could feel myself sliding in the mud. I tried to dig my heels in to gain footing and not lose any ground. I wanted to get one more shot. Instead my feet were swallowed by black oozing mud and my subject turned and ran.

While I worked at freeing myself, Jay was sitting in the truck, sipping his coffee, shaking his head, and chuckling. After escaping the mud, I was informed that I wasn't getting in his truck like that.

I sat down on the side of the road to rub my boots together. I was removing some of the caked on mud when I noticed a footprint. The impression hadn't come from a bear, or even a deer. The contours of the form were distinct and seemed to scream at me from the muddy surface: Wolf!

It was doubtful it was from a stray dog. There wasn't a house for miles, and the rangers always kept a sharp eye out for dogs that might harass the Red Wolves.

After Jay and I spent a few minutes examining the print, we saw another one. The sharpness of the prints indicated he wasn't running, but rather walking at a leisurely pace, and could still be in the area.

I followed the tracks along the side of the narrow dirt road, while Jay crept along in the truck behind me. Kneeling down, I stopped for just a moment to photograph one of the prints. There was a curve in the road up ahead. The wolf could be right around the bend. I motioned to Jay to stop while I slowly inched forward. From behind a bush I peeked around the bend to scan the area for any movement.

A sudden commotion startled me: I had been spotted. There was a splashing sound as a Great Blue Heron panicked. It cackled loudly, flapped its wings and took to the sky.

After a moment, I composed myself and continued on my quest. The prints diverted into the canal after rounding another curve in the road. I looked around the underbrush, scanned the mud for disturbances, and couldn't find any more prints.

Along the road were a series of open fields, and I could see for quite some distance. Jay and I scanned the landscape, but failed to find a single bear, deer, or wolf anywhere. We searched a little while longer hoping to find just one more paw print.

The gentle breeze that ruffled my hair carried with it a strange sound. Both Jay and I stopped and listened. At first it was faint and barely audible. Then, as we stood motionless on the side of the road, the sound grew louder, then louder still, until it became a chorus. The wolf had eluded us, but off in the distance he was signaling to his pack mates and they had joined his song.

As sunlight danced through the fields Jay and I knew we wouldn't be spotting any wolves today, so we took a few moments to just enjoy listening to their song.

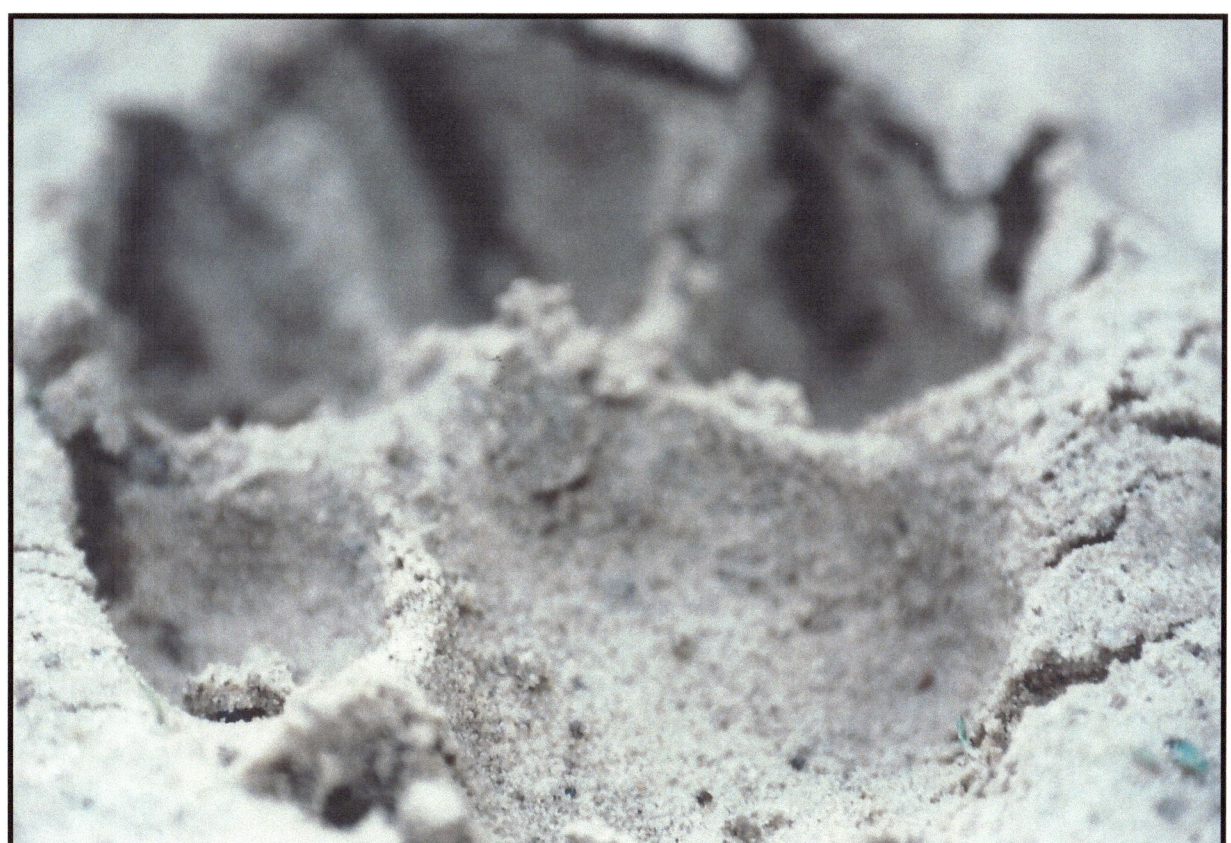

FEATHERS, FUR, AND SCALES

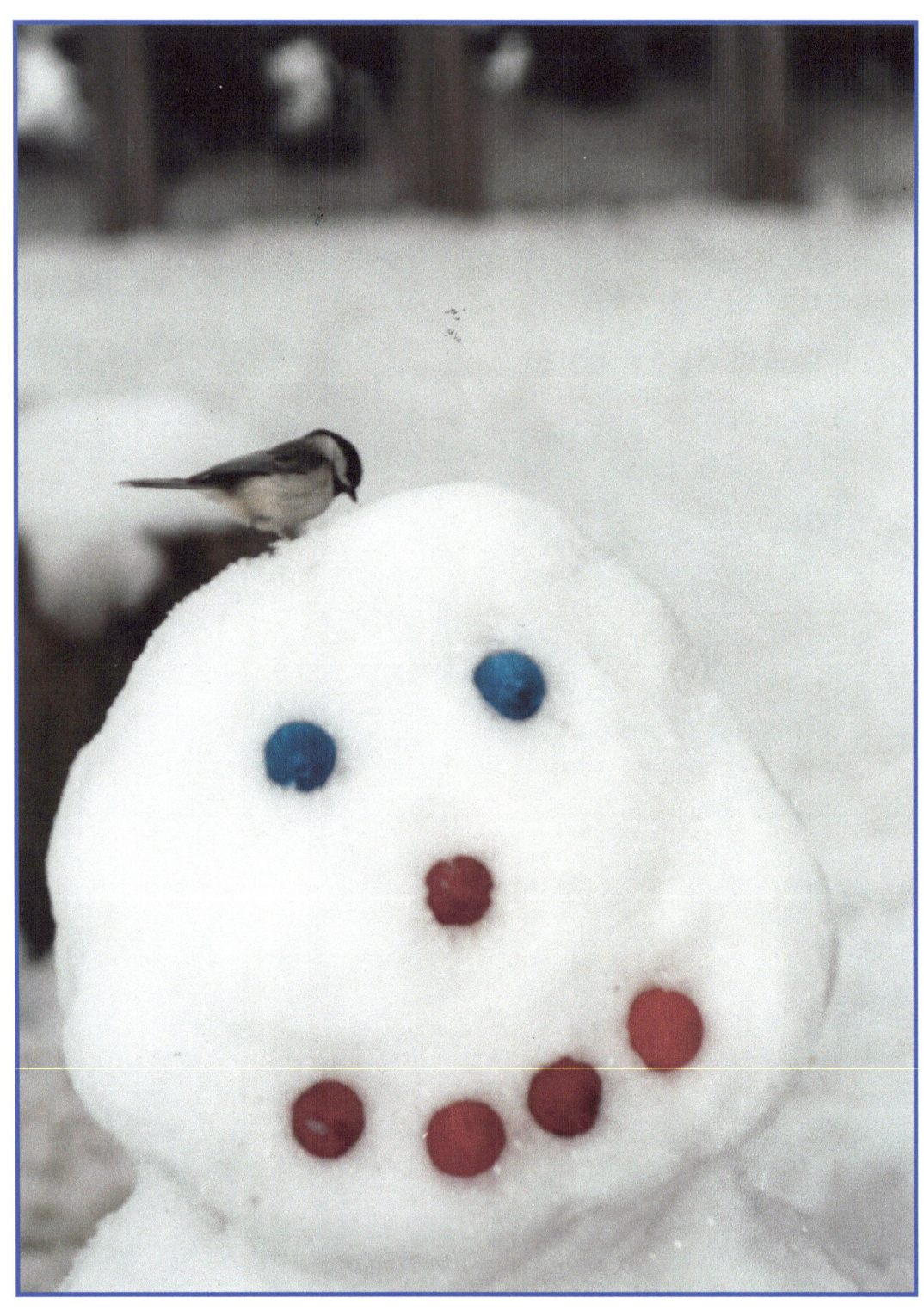

Winter arrived with a blast of arctic air. It seemed that literally overnight everything froze. Because of the frigid temperatures, most of my picture taking was restricted. I had discovered that once the camera batteries got too cold the camera simply wouldn't function. So my outdoor excursions were limited until the weather warmed up.

One afternoon, I decided to try something new. Instead of going out and seeing what I could find, my plan was to entice a few birds to pose for me. After all, we had a variety of birds that stayed in the area for the winter.

I wanted a few photographs of a bird visiting a snowman.

First, I bundled up and headed outside. After selecting a location, I began constructing a snowman. An hour later my snowman was finished, complete with birdseed sprinkled in a few spots.

Inside the kitchen, I placed my camera on the tripod near the window and waited, and waited.

Finally, a Blue Jay flew onto the snowman, quickly grabbed a sunflower seed, and left. A few minutes later, he returned.

The deep blue coloring of his back feathers cascaded into subtle shades of blue that faded into the cloudy gray feathers on his belly. Each time he darted back to retrieve a seed, I clicked off another frame.

Eventually, he absconded with all the sunflower seeds, so I bundled up, restocked the supply, and waited in vain for him to return.

After a while, I got tired of waiting, and went back to doing household chores.

I returned to the window several times, before spotting a Black Capped Chickadee on the snowman's head. As soon as I approached the camera, he headed for the shelter of a nearby bush. He hadn't gone far, so I was hoping he would return. I sat trying not to move. Eventually, my feathered friend landed on the snowman's head. Elated, I observed him pecking at the seed with his tiny, sharp beak. The deep black feathers on his head were ruffled by the wind as he enjoyed his meal. Happily, I snapped off frame after frame until he departed.

As the day wore on, the snowman was slowly engulfed by the shadow of the house. So I moved the camera to the front door. After taking a moment to clean the glass, I refilled the suet feeder in hopes of photographing a woodpecker.

Instead I spied a squirrel at the suet feeder. Now all I had to do was get to my camera without him seeing me.

The squirrel's thick gray coat was speckled with splashes of brown, and accented with white on his belly and on a single paw. Hanging by his tail, he grabbed the suet feeder with his tiny hand-like paw, retrieving a glob of suet. Holding his coveted prize close to his chest, he made his way onto a branch, and sat contently munching as the camera clicked away.

While he was preoccupied, I experimented with different angles and shutter speeds until I finished off the roll of film.

Feathers, Fur, and Scales

As winter slowly released its grip, lots and lots of rain replaced our weekly snowstorms. Faithfully, I checked the weather forecast hoping for a sunny morning. After weeks of waiting, the weatherman predicted a bright, sunny, spring day.

Jay and I made plans to be up early and head to the back roads. Our destination was the wildlife management area where we had camped before with friends.

When we arrived, we found a few Canada Geese wandering around. I wasn't sure if they had spent the winter or had recently arrived. They seemed unaccustomed to people, and weren't sure if they should flee or not. I took advantage of their hesitation, and clicked the shutter button before they waddled toward the safety of the water.

Zooming in on the pair through the lens, I could see the texture of the brown, black and white feathers that adorned their backs. I focused in on the black and white face of one of the geese.

He looked right at me.

I paused for a moment, before I clicked off another frame.

The larger of the two geese turned and began honking before plunging into the cold water. His big, black feet paddled beneath the surface, propelling him further away.

As we walked along, a large woodpecker flew by and landed in a nearby tree. The bright red crown of feathers on his head made him easy to observe while he darted from branch to branch. The rhythmic sound of his flapping wings echoed through the woods. He was much too active to photograph, but we enjoyed watching him.

A lone chipmunk scampered about in the leaves, probably looking for seeds. He paused for a moment on a log. Lying on the ground, I managed to capture the reddish brown critter on film. His tiny paws gripped the bark as he shook his long dark tail. The white lines that ran along the sides of his body became a blur when he scurried away.

After a few hours, we got back in the truck and headed down the mountain. As we traveled along the rugged dirt road, Jay saw what appeared to be a branch, and slowed down. In the road, basking in the warm sun was a large snake. I reached for the door handle.

"You're not going to get out are you?"

"Well, I can't get a very good picture from here, now can I?" was my reply.

Jay opted to stay in the truck with the windows rolled up. Snakes were one animal he just didn't like.

Bending down, I clicked the shutter button from a safe distance. Then, stepping forward, I got down on the ground with him.

"Hello. What are you doing in the road?"

As I peered through the lens, I could view the scales that ran along the snake's body. His golden yellow coloring gave way to geometric designs that decorated his entire body. The vertical pupils in his eyes gave him an intimidating appearance. Zooming in on him, I could see his tongue jetting in and out of his mouth.

"Do that again," I prompted.

As the camera clicked, I realized that this was a rattlesnake. These guys were poisonous.

I froze for a moment, trying to remember how far a snake could strike. Was it half the length of their body, or was it the length of their body? I couldn't remember. Either way, I was probably a bit to close.

I decided I had to keep the camera in front of me at all times. Most snakes will strike at whatever is closest to them. So if he did strike, hopefully, he would get the lens and not me. I just had to remember not to panic, and hold down the shutter button.

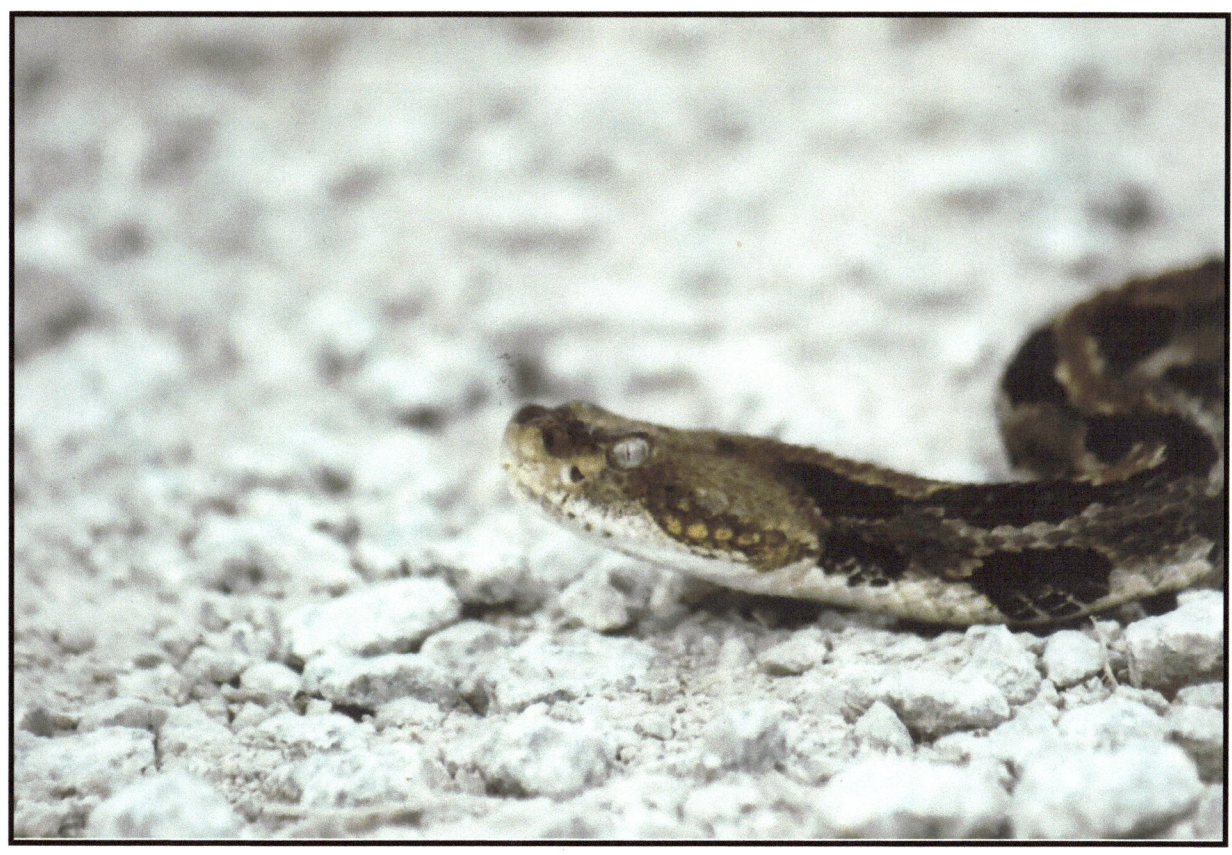

The snake slowly made its way to the side of the road. He then turned and looked right at me and began to rattle his tail. I knew he was no longer willing to tolerate me. Slowly, I crawled backwards while being careful not to make any sudden moves. I continued to press the shutter button during my retreat.

Once I was several feet away, I stood up and walked back to the truck. Jay shook his head and smiled. I was surprised when he asked,

"If the snake would have bitten you, would I need to take both you and the snake to the hospital, or just you?"

THE PLAYFUL PACHYDERM

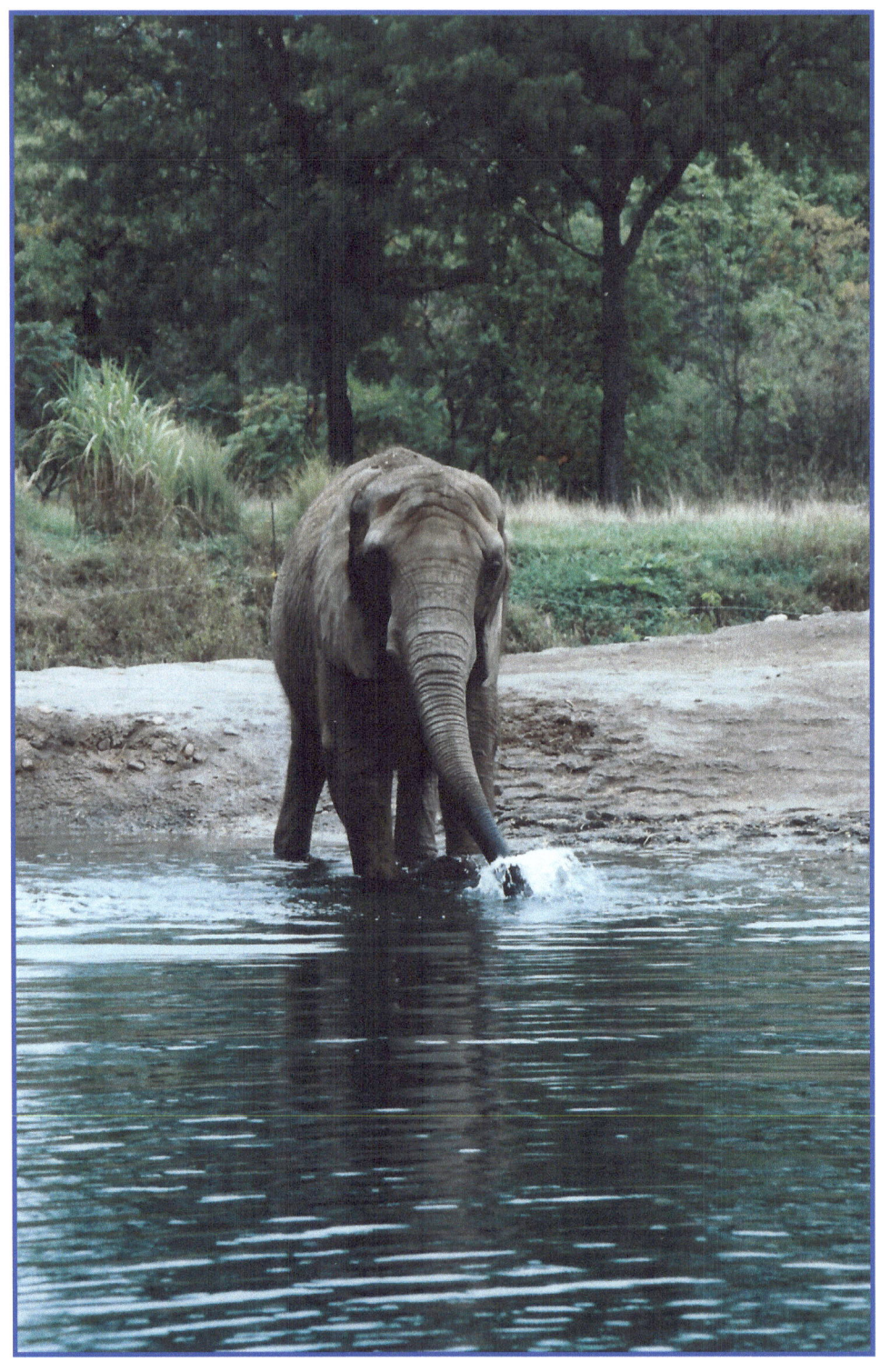

Imuch prefer photographing animals in the wild. I suppose it is the thrill of that one chance encounter, coupled with the challenge of getting it on film that makes it so exciting. However, I simply don't have the means to travel the world photographing wildlife, so occasionally Jay and I opt to visit a zoo.

After saving up a few dollars, we headed for a large zoo some distance from home. We arrived at our motel in time to get a good night sleep. During the night, the weather had deteriorated. It was quite cloudy and we suspected it would rain, but that was okay. There would be fewer people around and I could use my flash.

We had wandered around the zoo for an hour or so before stopping in front of the elephant enclosure. The elephants were separated from the public by a sturdy chain link fence and a wide moat.

I centered the camera lens on the fencing. Clouds of gray, brown and white shadows evolved into a group of elephants as I adjusted the focus and captured an image of the small herd.

Raindrops tapped my shoulder while I looked through the lens. The massive pachyderms wandered about while the camera clicked again and again.

One particular elephant seemed very interested in what I was doing. Perhaps he found the light from the flash appealing, or maybe he was simply curious. He wandered closer until eventually he made his way to the edge of the water in the moat.

"Somebody isn't camera shy."

I zoomed in on him as his giant foot broke the surface of the water. He splashed and played while I recorded his antics. These were shots I couldn't get every day, and I felt very lucky that he was posing for me. The enormous pachyderm was suddenly submerged. He resurfaced halfway across the moat and began swimming toward me.

"Hello, are you coming over to see me?"

I focused in on his thick, rough looking hide. He splashed about in the water with his trunk while I zoomed in on his face.

For a few minutes, I was totally unaware of what was going on around me. I was concentrating on my subject. I was getting some beautiful close up shots. He swam closer as the water rippled around him. I captured him from different angles as he approached. As he sprayed water from his agile trunk, there seemed to be a slight hint of mischief in his eyes. When he flapped his ears, I could hear the sound of them brushing the side of his head. He was so close I had to change to a smaller lens. Just as I finished someone tapped me on the shoulder.

"Excuse me. I'm sorry, but you're going to have to leave the area."

I looked up to find a zoo employee standing next to me.

"What?" I replied, surprised. "You have to leave now. You see that elephant has somehow managed to get on the other side of the cables that run through the moat. He obviously is coming to see you, and it isn't safe.

The Playful Pachyderm

We have to get him back where he belongs, and I don't think we can do that with you here. Could you please leave?" he pleaded.

I apologized for any trouble I may have caused, before Jay and I went to see the other animals.

During the course of our day, I was able to photograph a very grumpy Kodiak Bear. The size of his large feet amazed me; a single sharp claw was larger than my middle finger. The camera clicked away while he lounged on a rock ledge. His long thick coat was a blend of colors. Primarily dark brown, he was painted with light brown streams of color that accented his intimidating appearance. Wrinkling his pitch black nose, he snarled, signaling me that he wasn't a big fan of the flash, so we decided to leave him be.

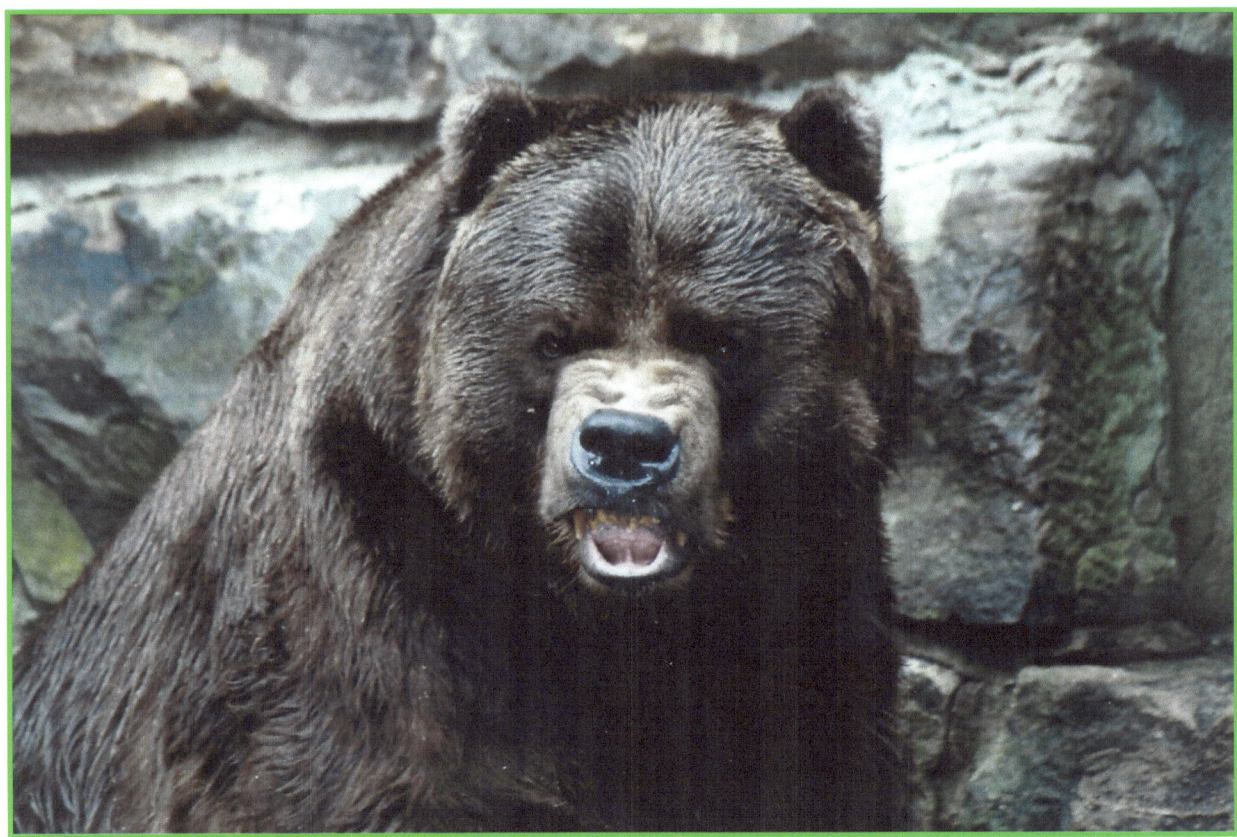

We paused to admire and photograph the giraffes. Their spindly legs and long necks made it difficult to get an entire giraffe in the lens. The brown patches that covered their bodies reminded me of jigsaw puzzle pieces.

As we made our way from one area to another, I captured an authoritative looking lion surveying his territory. The breeze ruffled his thick mane while he paced.

Then, we moved on to the primates. There we found a very vocal White Cheek Gibbon. An active member of the primate family, this playful monkey swung from branch to branch, announcing his presence. His black body was only a blur as he made his way across the enclosure. Finally, he paused, for just a moment. The white fur that accented his cheeks gave him an innocent looking appearance when I depressed the shutter button.

After this, Jay accompanied me into the reptile house. There was an array of snakes from all over the world. Although they were safely tucked behind glass, just being in the building made Jay nervous. He observed from a distance while I took shot after shot.

Before leaving for the day, we returned to the elephant enclosure. The mischievous pachyderm was safely on the other side of the half drained moat. Smiling, I waved to the nervous employees as they watched me walk by.

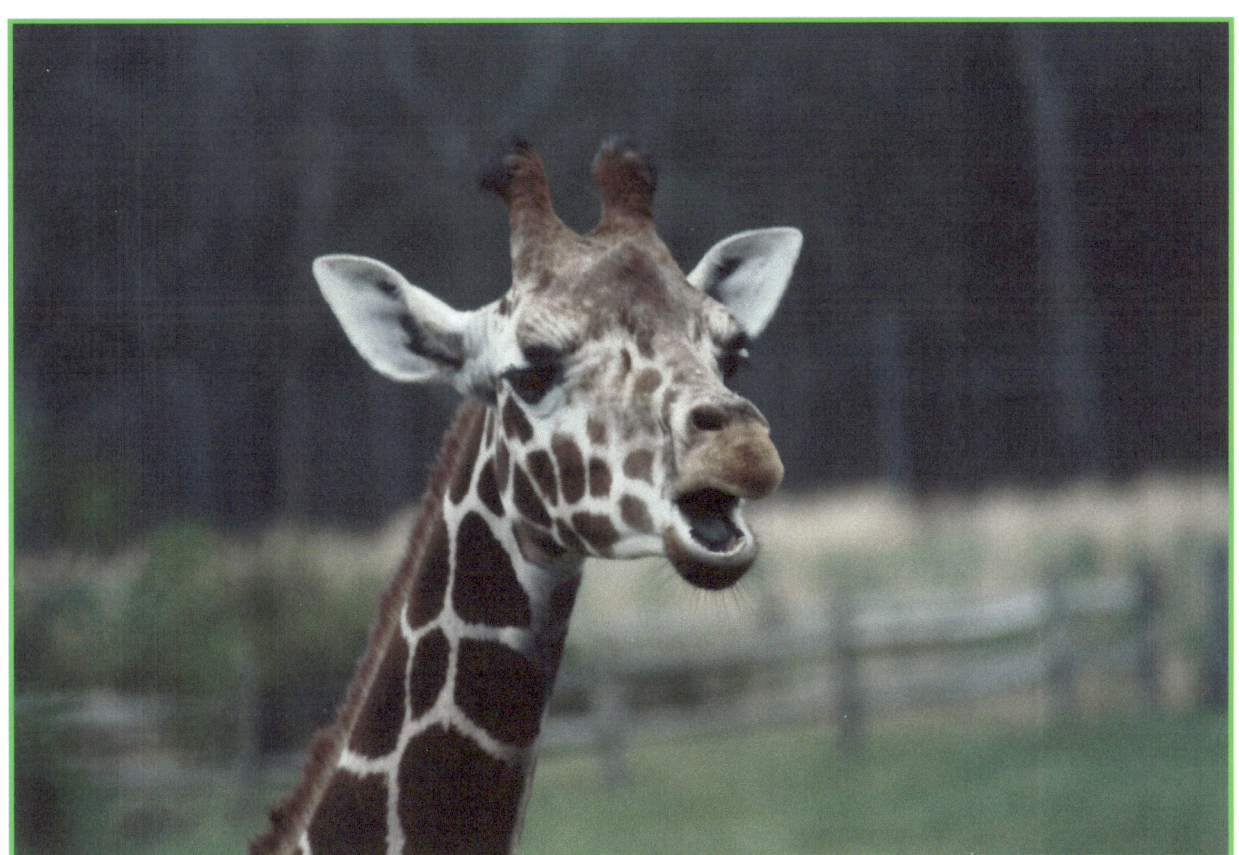

Camping Out

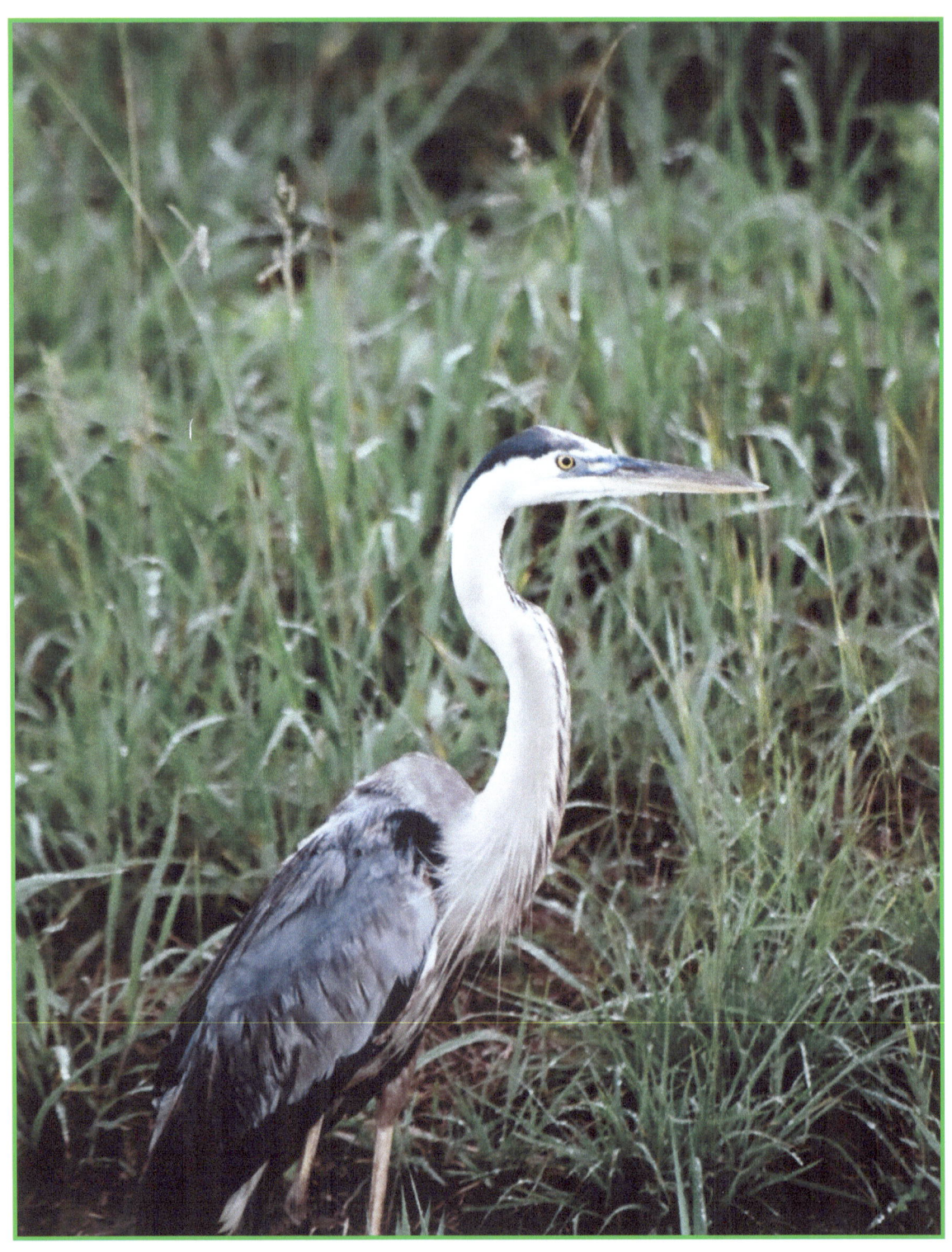

Wildlife management areas are well known to hunters, but few photographers take advantage of them out of season. I coordinated with a few friends, and headed to one to explore for a few days. It was a long, rough ride up and over the mountain, but eventually we arrived. Equipped with a few canoes, tents, coolers, and extra clothing, we set up camp near the lake. Our group consisted of me, Jay, George, and Sally. George was an experienced camper, while Sally was new to camping and anxious to learn all about the great outdoors. She did lose some of her enthusiasm when we explained there were no bathrooms, just an outhouse.

We set up our tents and collected firewood. Then the four of us went exploring in the woods. We followed one of the many deer trails that wove its way through the trees. Along the way George showed Sally hoof prints and paw prints that had been left in the trail. Carefully, he explained each print, helping her to identify what type of animal it belonged to. As we walked along, he also pointed out small tufts of hair that had been caught in the bark of a tree.

After an hour or so, we headed back to camp to start dinner. No fancy meals for this group, just hot dogs and beans cooked over an open fire.

Darkness descended while we sat by the fire and discussed our plans for the morning. The crackling of the fire echoed through the woods as a gentle breeze prompted the treetops to sway. The occasional hooting sounds of an owl drifted in the air. The skies had clouded over, and only the light from our campfire illuminated the area.

After roasting some marshmallows, we decided to get some sleep. We extinguished the fire and all went to our respective tents. Once the rustling of our sleeping bags ceased, I lay there for quite some time listening the sounds that surrounded me. A tree frog's call could be heard in the distance. Rhythmic snoring sounds emanated from of one of the other tents.

Then, a rustling noise in the leaves caught my attention. I listened to the sounds growing closer. Then, I heard clamoring and banging noises coming from right outside the tent. We definitely had a visitor. I wiggled my way around in the tent while trying not to wake Jay. Once I was facing the door flap, my trembling fingers slowly and quietly unzipped the tent.

Nervously, I peered out to scan the area for movement. I spotted a dark figure among the pots and pans. Staring intently, I tried to make out what it was. It was a raccoon searching for a morsel to eat. He made his way over to the coolers. His tiny hand-like paws fumbled at the catch. But the bungee cords we had secured around the cooler prevented him from getting to the food inside.

Coordinating my camera equipment and the spotlight, I fumbled around in the dark.

Then, I noticed a light coming from one of the other tents. Before I could react, the silence was broken by a blood-curdling scream.

The raccoon ran for cover as Sally babbled something about a giant creature.

"What's the matter? What's going on?" Jay yelled.

Camping Out

Soon we were all out of our tents and reassuring Sally that the raccoon wouldn't hurt her, he was only looking for a free meal.

Since I was up anyway, I made my way to the outhouse. Along the path, I spotted a mouse scurrying around in the leaves. A gentle breeze flowed through my hair as I walked. Off in the woods, I heard a slight noise. I pointed my flashlight in that direction, the light reflected in the eyes of a doe and she froze.

"Hello. We're just visiting and we'll be gone tomorrow evening. "

The deer suddenly bolted deeper into the woods and I proceeded to the outhouse.

Back at camp, Sally had finally settled down, and was safely in her tent with the flashlight on. George and Jay both had also returned to their tents. As they lay in their sleeping bags, they talked back and forth while teasing Sally about being attacked by a killer raccoon.

In the morning, the sounds of a crackling fire woke me. The aroma of fresh brewed coffee tickled my nostrils, and mixed with the smell of sausage. I quickly dressed and joined George by the fire. Jay was out collecting more firewood, and Sally was fast asleep.

The air had a damp chill to it, and we suspected it would rain, but we didn't care. Along with our provisions, we had all packed rain gear.

Jay returned to camp with an armload of firewood just as Sally made her way out of the tent.

"Coffee, I need coffee, and a shower," she moaned.

"Drink up, then go get in the lake," George laughed while handing her a cup.

Over breakfast, we divided up the chores, and decided to take down our tents before the rain started. By mid-morning, we had the canoes in the water and were packing them with supplies. Our camping gear was safely locked in the truck, and we were ready to start paddling.

Sitting in the front of our boat, I nervously directed Jay around the stumps that protruded from the surface of the water. The water gently lapped at the sides of the boat as we headed for deeper water. In the distance songbirds chattered to each other. Through the mist, the opposite shore of the lake was barely visible.

After a few moments, I adjusted my lifejacket and began to relax and enjoy our surroundings. Retrieving my camera from its home in a spackle bucket, I scanned the area for movement.

As we drifted along, we spotted a beaver dam off one of the more secluded banks.

A large floating mass of water lilies slowly engulfed us while we drifted. I wanted to get a picture of one of the flowers that was blooming. Jay thought I should simply snap the picture, but I wanted to set up the shot. After all, the flower wasn't going anywhere. Jay leaned to the right to balance the boat while I leaned to the left. Through the lens, I focused in on the dark green lily pads that gently surrounded the bright white flower. While I was adjusting the shutter speed, Jay suddenly leaned to the left nearly tossing me out of the boat. As I fumbled to stay in the boat my finger depressed the shutter button several times, finishing off the roll of film.

While I reloaded the camera, Jay spotted a large bird in the distance. Paddling toward it, we saw the white coloring of its neck and chest. She shook her dark brown wings and ruffled her back feathers. Its bright piercing eyes watched our every move. It was an osprey; she had perched on an old tree stump. Jay paddled closer as I focused the camera and I clicked off a picture of her. As we neared the nervous bird, we realized the osprey had landed on its nest, not just a tree stump with branches on it.

As we drifted closer, I zoomed in on the nest and discovered the osprey was not alone. Then, with a sudden flap of her wings, she was soaring over our heads screeching. I clicked off another frame when she passed over me. Leaning further and further back, I followed her with the lens of the camera and clicked off shot after shot.

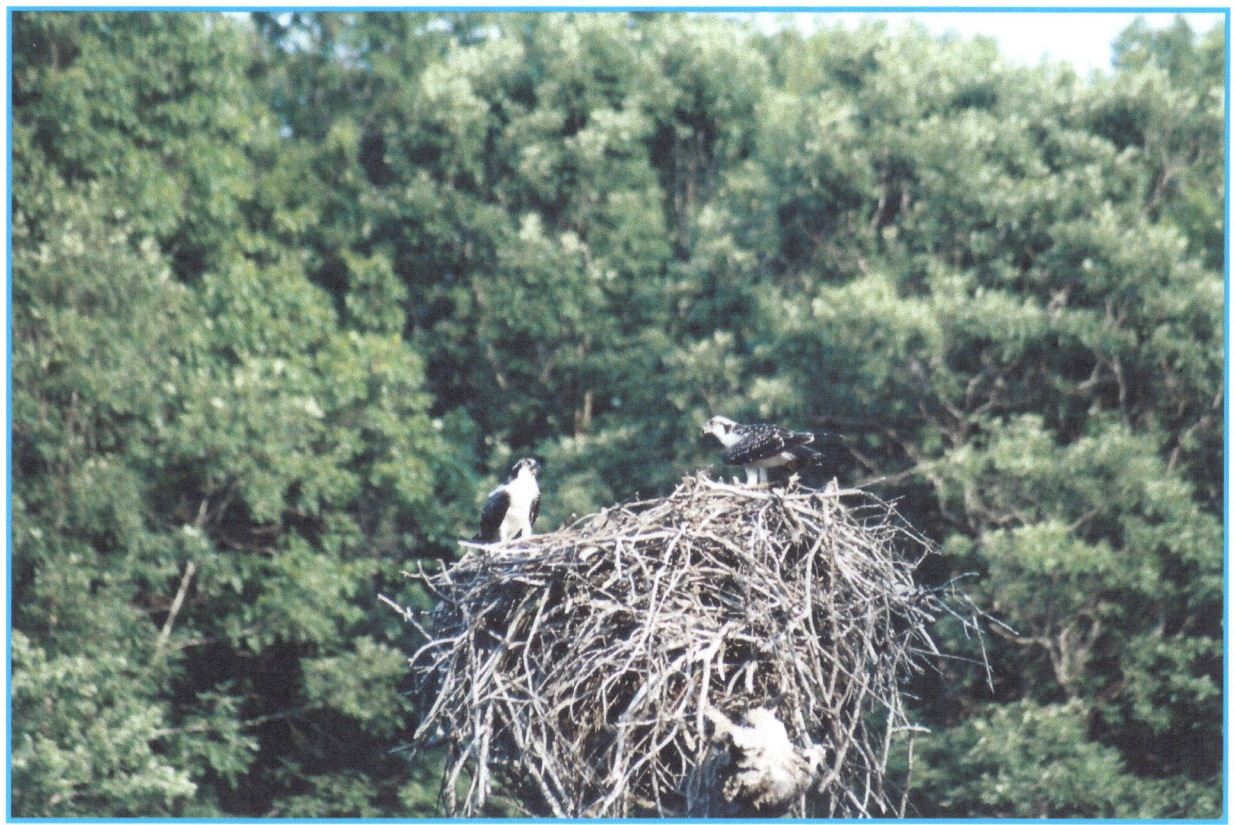

Not far ahead of us, floating quietly, were a few Canada Geese. Through the lens, I could see the soft feathers that covered their bodies. They began to honk loudly when we approached. I zoomed in and snapped a picture just as they left the surface of the water and took to the sky. It was obvious the animals here were used to hunters and were a bit skittish.

We joined George and Sally on the shore for lunch. While we dined under an old tree, it began to rain. Undeterred, we put on our rain gear and proceeded back to the canoes.

As I was snapping the lid on the spackle bucket, a heron flew by and landed nearby. Jay and I made our way through the trees and slowly ventured toward him. The heron stood motionless for a moment, deciding if we were threat. Then he slowly spread his wings, preparing to take flight. I peered through the lens and clicked the shutter button as Jay whispered in my ear, "Take the shot, take the shot."

The rain had slowed to a steady mist, as we paddled the canoe along the shore line.

Off in the woods, Jay heard a rustling sound. When I glanced over, I saw movement in one of the trees. The rustling continued as we approached. Whatever it was, it seemed unaware of our presence when we inched the canoe onto the shore. I carefully stood up and stepped one foot out of the canoe onto dry land.

Just as I lifted the other leg, Jay whispered to me, "Get back in the boat."

"What?"

"Get back in the boat. It could be a bear cub, and then Mom won't be far away."

Camping Out

I sat back down and we watched the leaves of the tree move about quickly. I really wanted to go see what it was. For what seemed like an eternity we sat and watched. Jay was right; it could be dangerous to wander into the woods pursuing an unknown animal.

Suddenly Jay exclaimed, "Do you believe that? It's a couple of squirrels!"

My hopes of getting a photo of a bear were dashed. The squirrels were too far off for me to get a decent picture. So we paddled back out into the lake and met George and Sally. It was now past four, we were all cold and wet, and so we headed toward home. George promised to take the scenic route and give us a complete tour of the area, but he wanted to be off the mountain by dark.

Once the canoes were tied securely on the truck, we all changed into dry clothes, and left the campsite.

Along the way, a flock of turkeys crossed our path. Carefully, I exited the truck. Using the vehicle to conceal the birds' view of my approach, I clicked off a few frames. Their sharp beaks protruded from the scaly looking flesh that encompassed their small heads. As I stepped closer, I was spotted and the group retreated into the woods and quickly vanished.

Along the way, we spotted some turtles on the edge of a small pond. While the sunlight danced on the water, I lay on the ground, and framed in their smooth-looking shells. With a splash, the wary turtles plunged into the water and out of sight.

We arrived home as the sun was beginning to set. It had been a good trip, a little wet, but good just the same. George, Jay, and I had enjoyed the quick encounters we had experienced. Sally, on the other hand, decided that she could manage to get through life without ever going camping again.

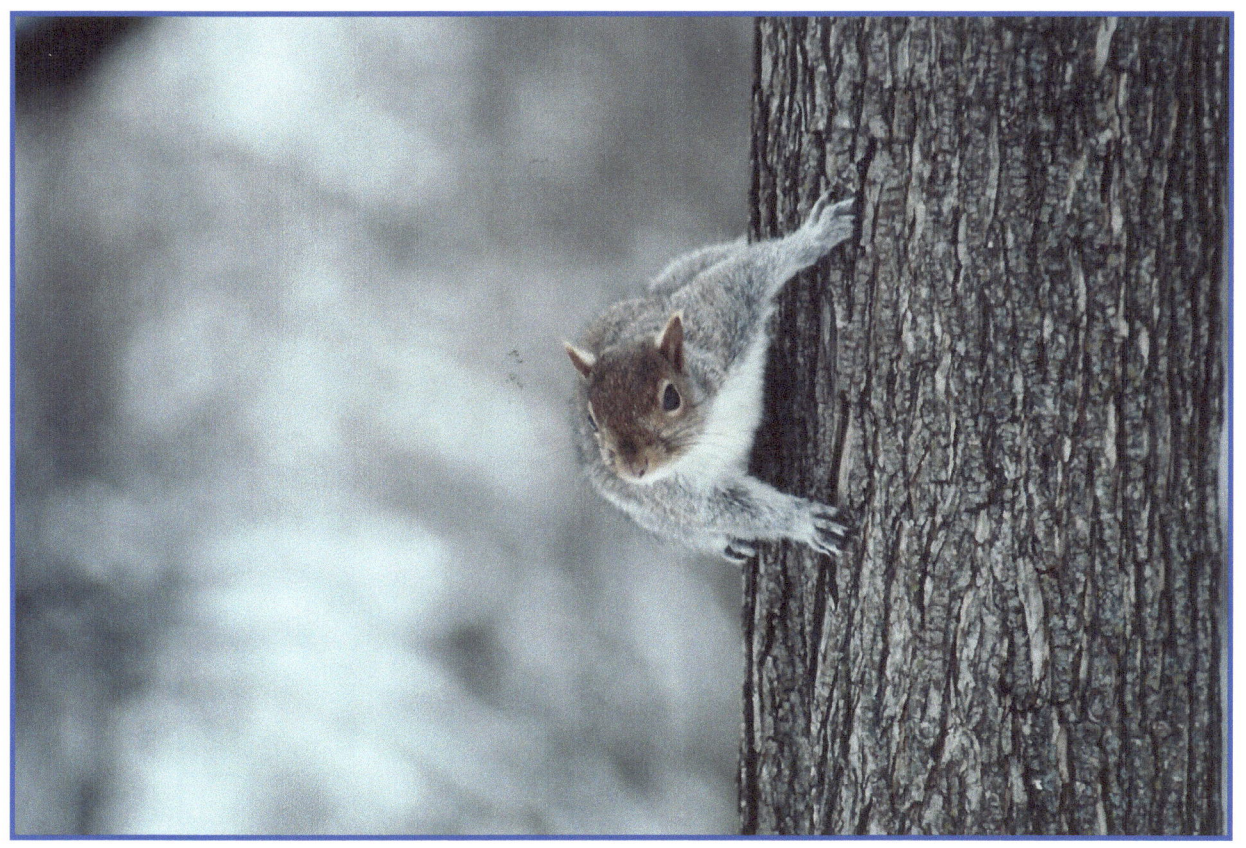

PHOTOGRAPHIC MEMORIES

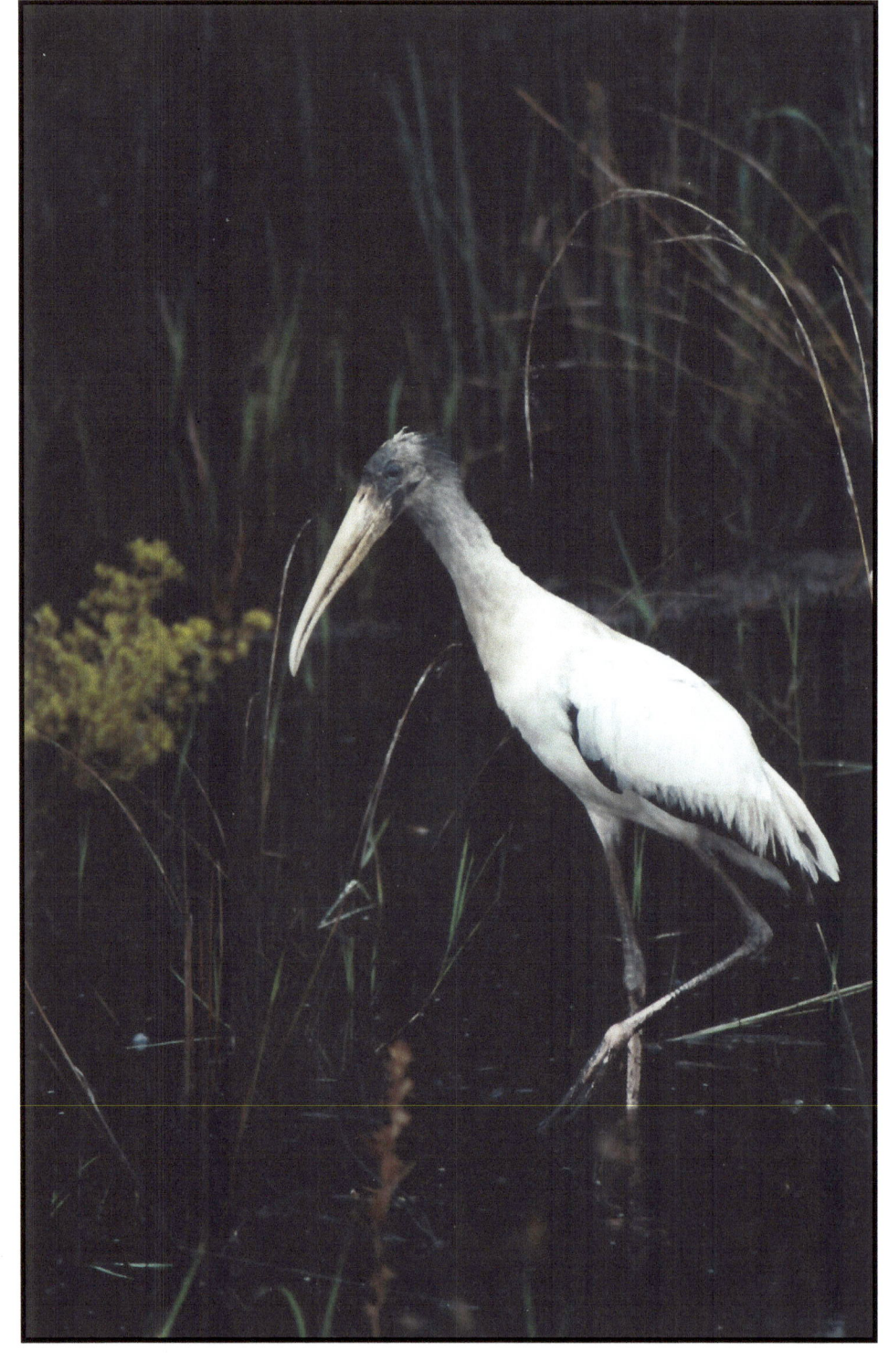

The thrill of an animal encounter is my favorite part of being a wildlife photographer. Since I shoot with film, there is also the task of numbering each photograph, then examining them and weeding out the not-so-good shots. Although I am diligent about numbering my prints, I often let them stack up before sorting through them to find the really good shots. That's what rainy days at home are for.

One such rainy afternoon, I sat with a stack and looked through each photograph. Viewing the close-up shots of the huge alligator, I recalled the lecture I got from Jay about paying attention to what I was doing. After all, my mother would never forgive him if I got eaten by an alligator.

There were pictures I had taken while we were on the air boat ride in Florida. My sister Betty and her husband, Ray, joined us that day. Betty and I weren't thrilled with being on a boat, but were excited about the animals we might see.

While the air boat skimmed across the surface of the water, our tour guide pointed out manatees in the water. I had seen manatees on television, but had never actually seen one in person before. These huge, slow-moving animals were a bit peculiar looking, and it was obvious to me why they are also known as sea cows. The large gray bodies of the manatees drifted along slowly, just below the surface of the water. Most of them had visible scars from close calls with boats in the area. Occasionally, one of them would surface and I would catch a glimpse of their gentle faces. All too soon we left the area and headed further down the river.

We were maneuvering through the shallow water when Jay spotted a Bald Eagle, then another. Quietly, the boat drifted toward one of the majestic raptors. Jay pointed out his location, while I captured him on film. When we neared the bank, the eagles took flight. In another location, we stopped so that I could photograph a group of pelicans perched on a small island.

Then, we spotted these large black birds standing along the bank. These unusual looking birds were covered with dull black feathers except for a patch of white under their chins. Their thick dark beaks flapped as we floated by. They stood motionless with their wings spread, basking in the afternoon sun.

Later, I learned these Anhingas were quite common in this area. I had managed to get a few good shots of the Anhingas, but only one was a good vertical shot.

Sorting through my photographs, I came to the images I had taken in Georgia.

While driving along a back road early one morning, Jay and I spotted a wood stork. His home was in a marshy area along the road. He carefully stepped on his long, thin legs in the muddy area. He explored the murky water with his long yellow beak.

I cautiously moved toward him. Once on his side of the road, I bent down and got him into frame. He wasn't the least bit interested in me. Moving closer, I zoomed in for a vertical image. Surprised at how close I was, I marveled at how the dark feather on its head slowly faded into the while feathers that covered the stork's body. After taking several photographs, we left him there wandering on the side of the road. Out of the numerous photos I had of this unattractive, but co-operative critter, I picked the three I liked the most to add to my portfolio.

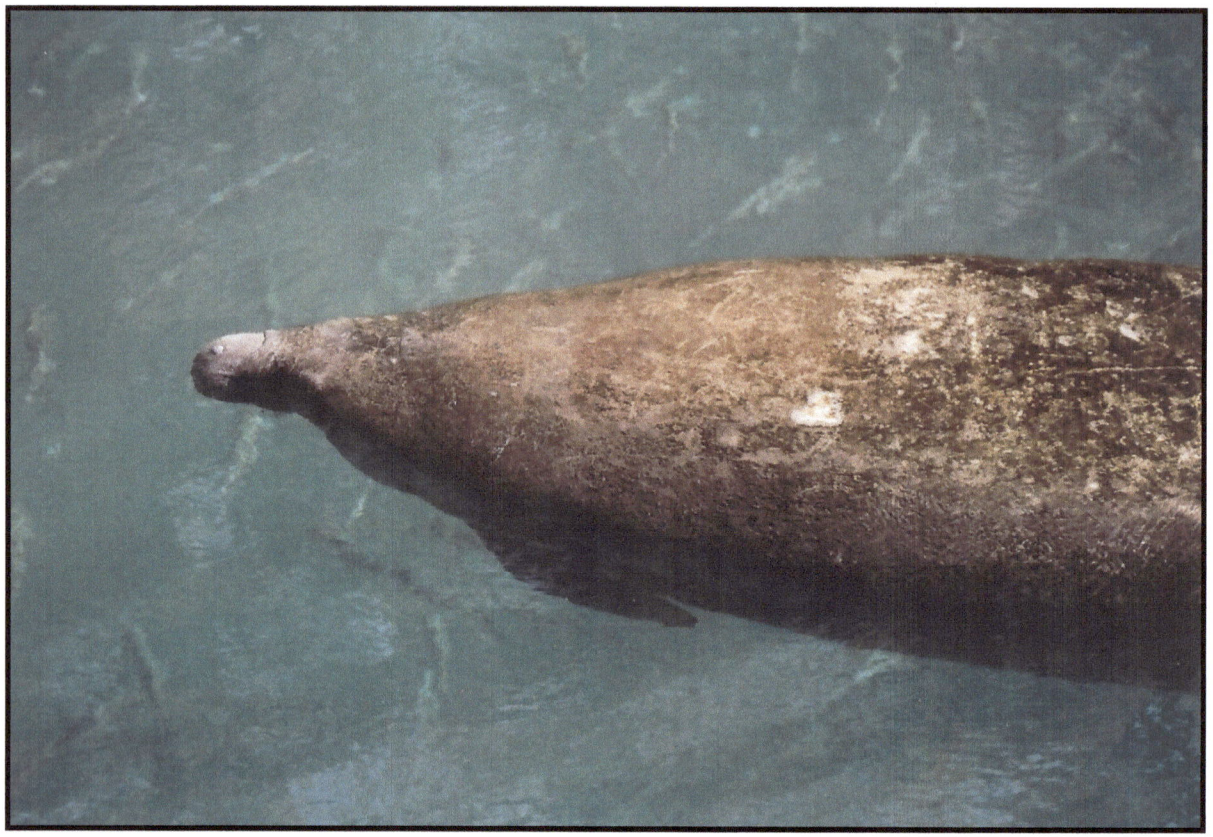

Next were images of captive critters.

I had managed to get some great shots of a hippopotamus in the water. As he swam around in a large pond, I simply sat outside the fence with my camera zoomed in and ready for him. Then, with a quick snap, I had him.

A little while later, I was able to get a few more shots while one of the keepers fed him. His huge gaping mouth contained an array of thick teeth of various lengths. The pink interior of his mouth matched the areas around his eyes and ears. All of these features combined to make a nice portrait of the hippopotamus.

The photographs from one of our afternoon excursions made their way to the top of the stack. On a whim, Jay and I had put the canoe on the truck on a sunny afternoon and headed just a few miles up the road. We arrived at the historic stone bridge that passed over a small creek. This would be our starting point.

Soon, we were paddling along in a world of our own. A mix of aromas from a variety of wildflowers filled the air. We slowly drifted past a turtle on a fallen tree.

Then we saw a small flock of Canada Geese gathered along the bank. We paddled toward them. Just as I raised my camera, they began making a terrible racket and quickly left the area.

The chattering of a kingfisher could be heard in front of us. Jay scanned the trees on one side, while I checked the other. Suddenly, Jay grabbed his paddle and began paddling.

"Get ready, I'm going to take you right under it," he whispered.

While focusing, I noticed his deep blue feathers came to a point on his head. A band of white feathers ran around his neck, while patches of white and chestnut brown formed a design on his belly. His long sharp beak seemed the perfect tool for eating fish. Quickly, I took his picture before he flew a few hundred yards ahead of us. As we paddled toward him, I saw a Great Blue Heron close to where he had landed. Quietly, we drifted along while I tried to find the heron in my lens. He wasn't happy about our presence and flew around the bend of the creek.

Water trickled into the creek from a small stream, as we searched for the birds. The kingfisher's cackle taunted us from a distance.

We rounded the bend; there along the bank was the heron, carelessly poking in the mud. We floated toward it and I nervously positioned my camera. A slight breeze fanned his feathers as I focused. Then, I depressed the shutter button and captured him.

Further up the creek, we found a large tree had fallen, and blocked our path. We got out of the canoe and surveyed the situation.

Trudging through the knee-deep water, we pulled and prodded the canoe. With a splash, a paddle landed in the water. Eventually, we lifted the canoe over the obstacle and we continued on our journey.

Before long, we could hear the sounds of cars passing over the nearby bridge. We knew our leisurely afternoon trip was about over. We had hoped to spot the heron or the kingfisher again, but neither of them seemed to be in the area. We floated to the bank and began emptying the canoe.

Suddenly the kingfisher zoomed past, chattering and announcing his presence.

There weren't many really good shots from this last section of the stack. I found myself discarding a few blurry shots of the kingfisher, along with a shot of the muddy banks, and two totally out of focus shots of the Canada Geese taking flight.

The end result was a much smaller stack of photographs to be added to my portfolio.

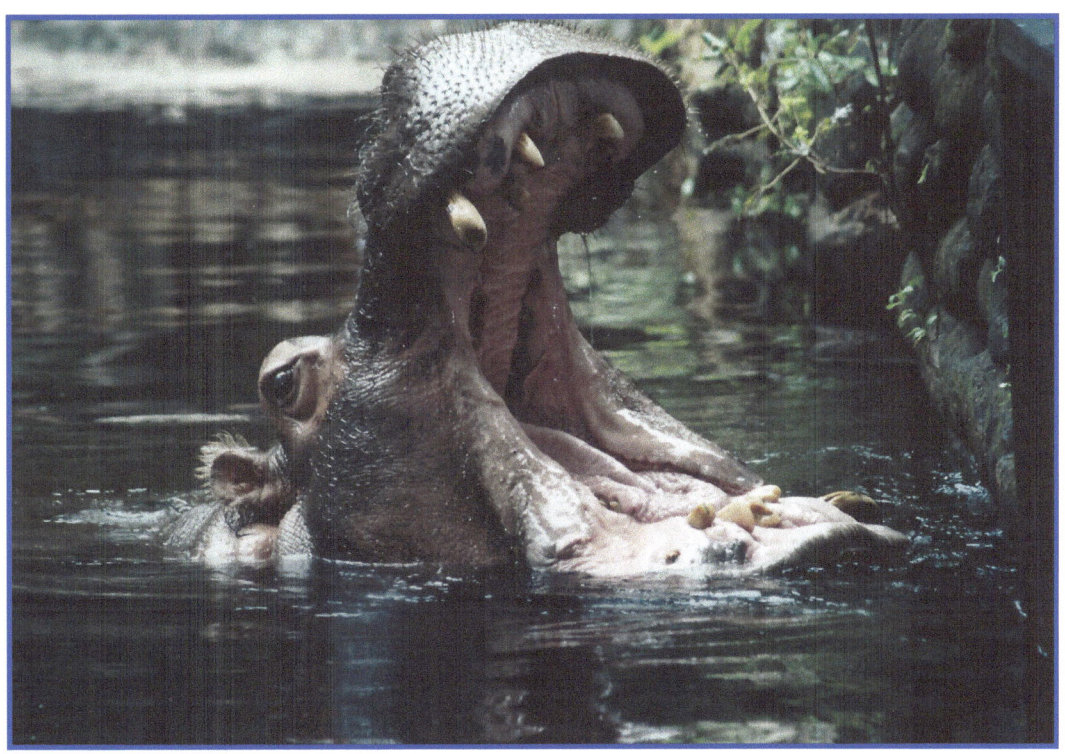

A New Project

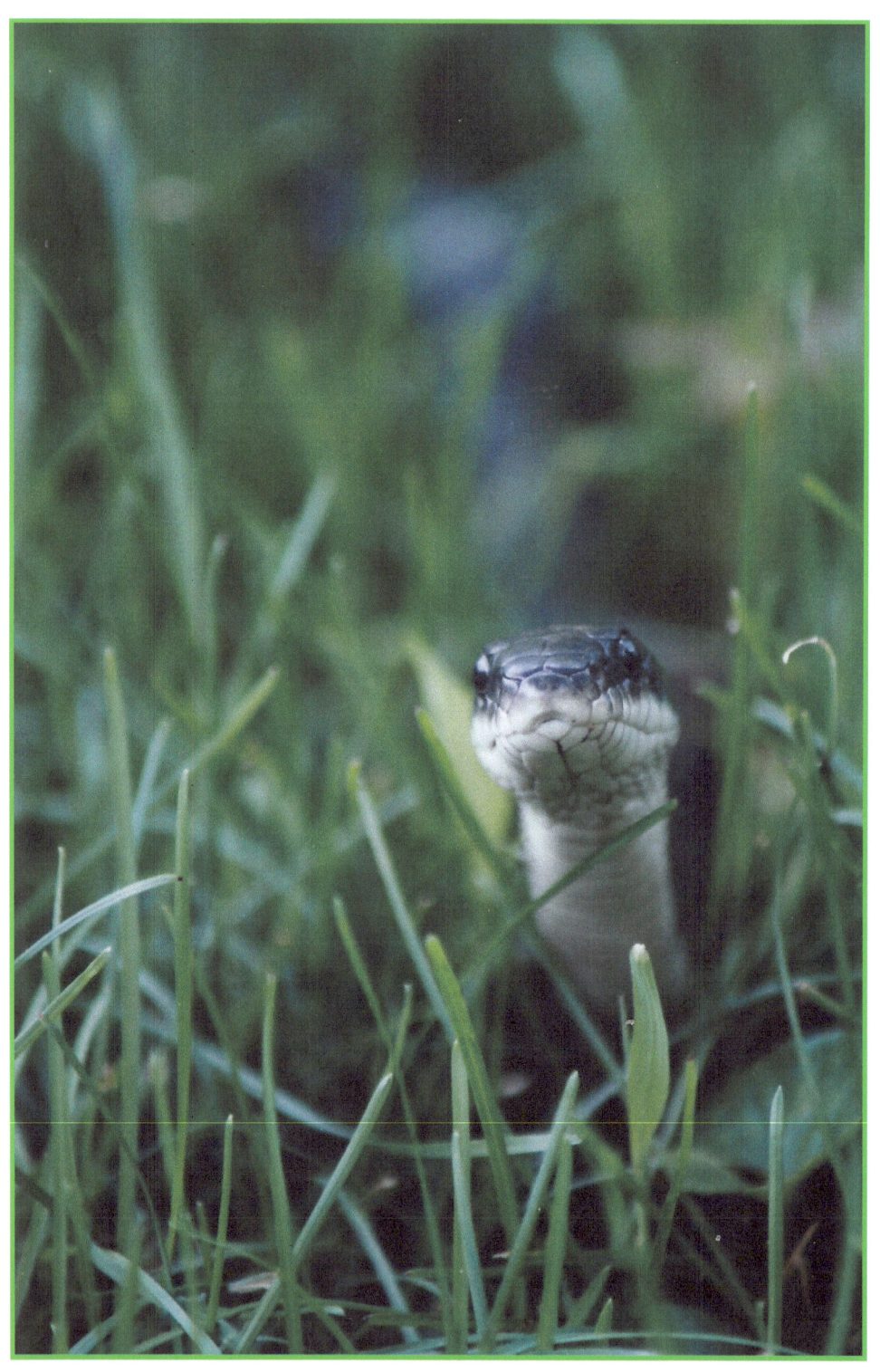

I had been invited to join a local writers group, and I was curious about how it worked. So, a few weeks later I found myself sitting at a large table with a number of writers at the local library.

By the time the meeting ended, I had decided that it was time to tackle a new project. It was an idea I had been playing with for some time, a book about wildlife in people's back yards. Maybe this odd mixture of writers could help me get started.

My initial attempts at the book resulted in a blank computer screen, but then the project quickly took on a life of its own. I started by spending hours photographing in my backyard. I wanted my book to include not simply the butterflies that visited, but also the delicate flowers that attracted them.

Each chapter of my book was devoted to a different backyard. At a friend's home, hummingbirds buzzed past my head. There were several of these tiny, swift birds that spent their summers with her. For a moment I observed them, before capturing their long thin beaks, beautiful green coloring, and swift wings. Three rolls of film later, I headed home, eager to start on the next chapter.

A neighbor who had heard about my book project insisted that I accompany her to visit some friends. Once there, I explained the project I was working on to this friendly couple, and they were happy to give me a tour of their property.

Along the way, they pointed out different native plants and herbs, and then stood back while I took photographs. The size of the giant, green leaves that sheltered the tiny yellow blooms on the dock plants surprised me. Hidden beneath an evergreen, there was a collection of shade loving plants and a tiny delicate spider. Unfortunately, I couldn't capture him on film, but the plants photographed beautifully.

During our tour, a snake fell from a nearby tree. Although my neighbor was startled, I was delighted. I lay down on the ground, and zoomed right in on his face. He eagerly approached the lens while I focused. This was the image I was looking for. Click, click went the camera as he made his way across the grass. Slowly, he turned his narrow dark body and glided up a tree.

Over lunch, we chatted about the animals they welcomed. Along with snakes; there were birds, both large and small; deer; and even an occasional fox. The beaver that had taken up residence here had built a dam and flooded a portion of the yard, but they lived here too, so the family simply adapted to the change in landscape and enjoyed watching the beavers frolic in the evenings.

I could have stayed there for days, exploring and photographing, but soon it was time to go. I had some new friends, a lot of information for the book and an invitation to return anytime.

Not long after that excursion, I had a phone call from another neighbor, Chris. He insisted I needed to bring my camera to his house right away. When I arrived, he was waiting for me by the fishpond. Beside him was a large frog, whose big yellow eyes stared up at me with apprehension. He sat motionless while I inched toward him and knelt down. The plump green frog allowed me to only take a few shots before he retreated into the pond.

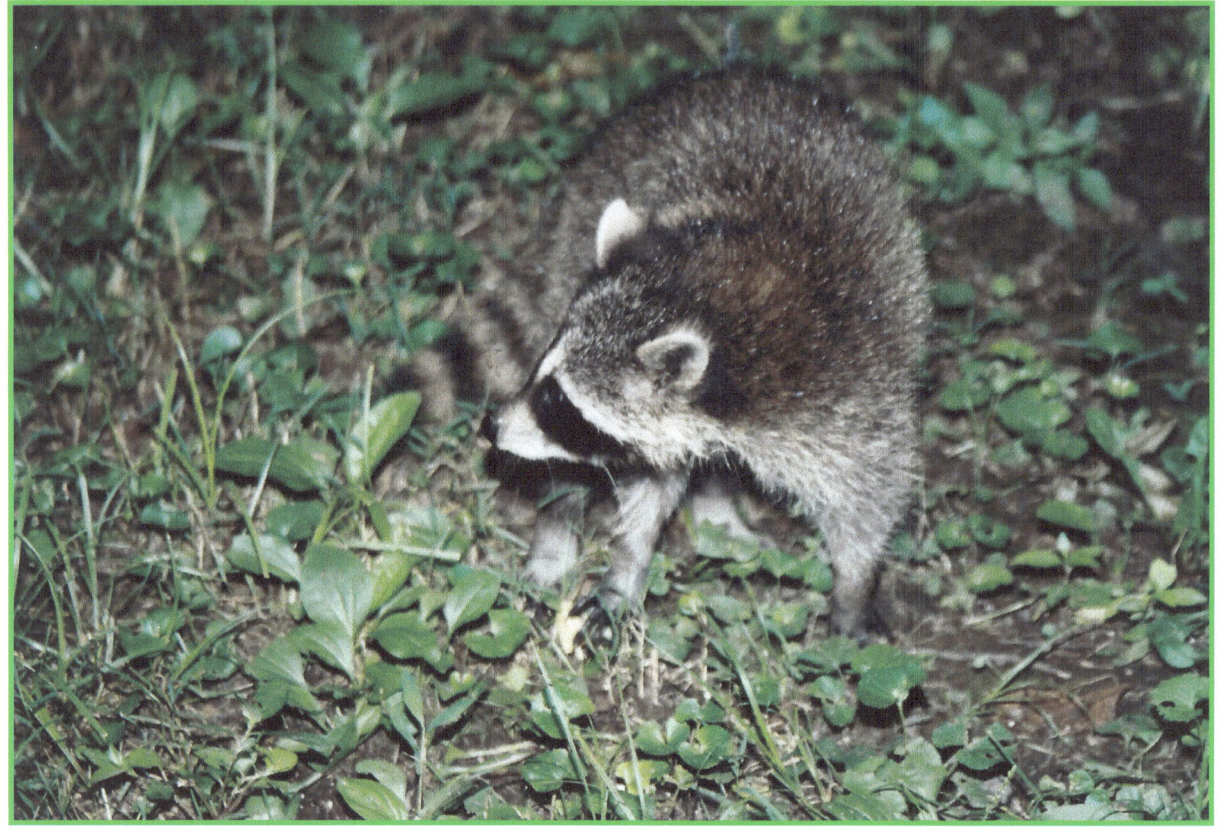

I noticed the variety of plants, flowers and bird feeders that had been arranged in this small backyard. Over by the garage, the clematis was in full bloom. Pastel purple lines ran through the center of each white petal. The numerous blooms accented the yard beautifully. A variety of bird feeders were near the walkway.

While I was talking with Chris, a Robin tugged at a worm. The tiny worm wiggled with all his might trying to get free from the determined Robin. Slowly, I turned, knelt down and zoomed in on the struggle. Just as I was about to click the shutter button, the Robin gave up the fight and departed. Soon, I was adding this backyard to the book.

I was accumulating a wide variety of photographs and information. After completing each chapter, I presented it to the group for assistance. Page by page, my book was coming together.

The next backyard was discovered on an out of town trip to visit with family. On the side of the road was a sign for a quaint sounding restaurant, so we stopped for lunch. The establishment was a log cabin with large windows and a friendly staff. While waiting for our meal, birds flew to and from feeders placed outside the windows.

I retrieved my camera from the truck.

A bright red cardinal flew onto the feeder. Sunlight danced on his feathers as the camera clicked. At the next table, I could hear a family discussing the types of birds they were seeing. A Black Capped Chickadee flew in for a bite to eat. As he pecked at the seeds, I focused in on the dark black coloring that adorned the top of his head and clicked the shutter button. I refocused the camera and framed in his tiny sharp beak just as he picked up a seed. When our food arrived, I was still busy photographing the birds.

During a brief conversation with the owner, I learned that the food may have brought most of their customers here, but the birds were also part of the restaurant's appeal.

This was yet another yard for the book.

A few weeks later, I was selling my photographs at a show when a woman stopped and inquired about photographs of raccoons. Three nights later, I was observing two baby raccoons she and her husband had rescued a few months before. The raccoons were now living in the woods by her home. Each evening, when she returned from work, she fed grapes, berries, or other fruits to them.

Since the two brothers weren't used to strangers, I kept my distance while observing them for a few minutes. Slowly, I made my way onto the deck to watch and photograph the raccoons from off to the side.

The hum of the cameras motor as it rewound the roll of film enticed one of the brothers to come investigate my camera and me. Carefully, I put a new roll of film in the camera while he approached. I sat quietly, smiling as he probed the camera with his tiny paws, before pressing his nose against the lens. I clicked the shutter button, and I chuckled at his antics. I couldn't believe I was this close to a wild animal. Although my pulse was racing and I was really excited, I tried to move as little as possible, not wanting to scare him.

His soft fur brushed against my hand as he explored the pockets of my camera bag. His brother was busy washing and eating grapes, and wasn't the least bit curious about their visitor. I found myself clicking off three rolls of film before the raccoons finished their meal. Slowly, they made their way off the deck, along the lawn, and back into the woods and out of sight.

Every few weeks, I headed back to the writers group with my latest pages. One afternoon, after the meeting, one of the members mentioned she had a friends who lived on eighty acres of land. She thought they would be a good addition to the book. As soon as I got home, I contacted her friends and made plans to visit.

The prospect of exploring eighty acres enticed Jay to accompany me on this outing. We met our hosts and enjoyed a few minutes of casual conversation before they escorted us around the property. The pond they had added years before was a big attraction to a family of beavers, as well as a variety of birds large and small, but none of them wanted to be photographed.

We followed a rugged dirt path through the woods. Zigzagging our way along, we crossed a small creek by balancing ourselves on a crudely constructed log bridge. This more secluded area of the property hid a variety of animals. Beside the path, Jay spied a box turtle munching on some vegetation. His thick hard shell was concealed beneath the leaves and only his head was visible. His sharp beak-like jaw clamped down on a wild strawberry. I positioned myself on the ground, peered through the lens, and clicked off a few shots before leaving him to enjoy his meal. We saw signs that deer had visited the area, and our hosts had even heard a bobcat on occasion.

As we stood by the house, a hawk flew into a nearby tree. He obviously didn't feel threatened since he allowed me to walk right up to the base of the tree. I could feel my heart pounding when I moved the camera to my face. The large leaves of the old oak tree partially concealed my view of him. Slowly, I repositioned myself trying to find a good angle for the camera. He turned his head and watched every move I made. A gentle breeze ruffled his dark brown feathers as I focused in on him, only to find another leaf right in the way. After putting up with me for several minutes, the hawk decided to look elsewhere for a free meal. With a sudden flap of his wings, he was airborne. I watched him soared over the pond and out of sight.

Our hosts relayed several stories to me about their animal encounters. Before our visit ended, I had lots and lots of material for yet another chapter in my book. The hardest part of writing this book would be deciding what not to include.

River Excursion

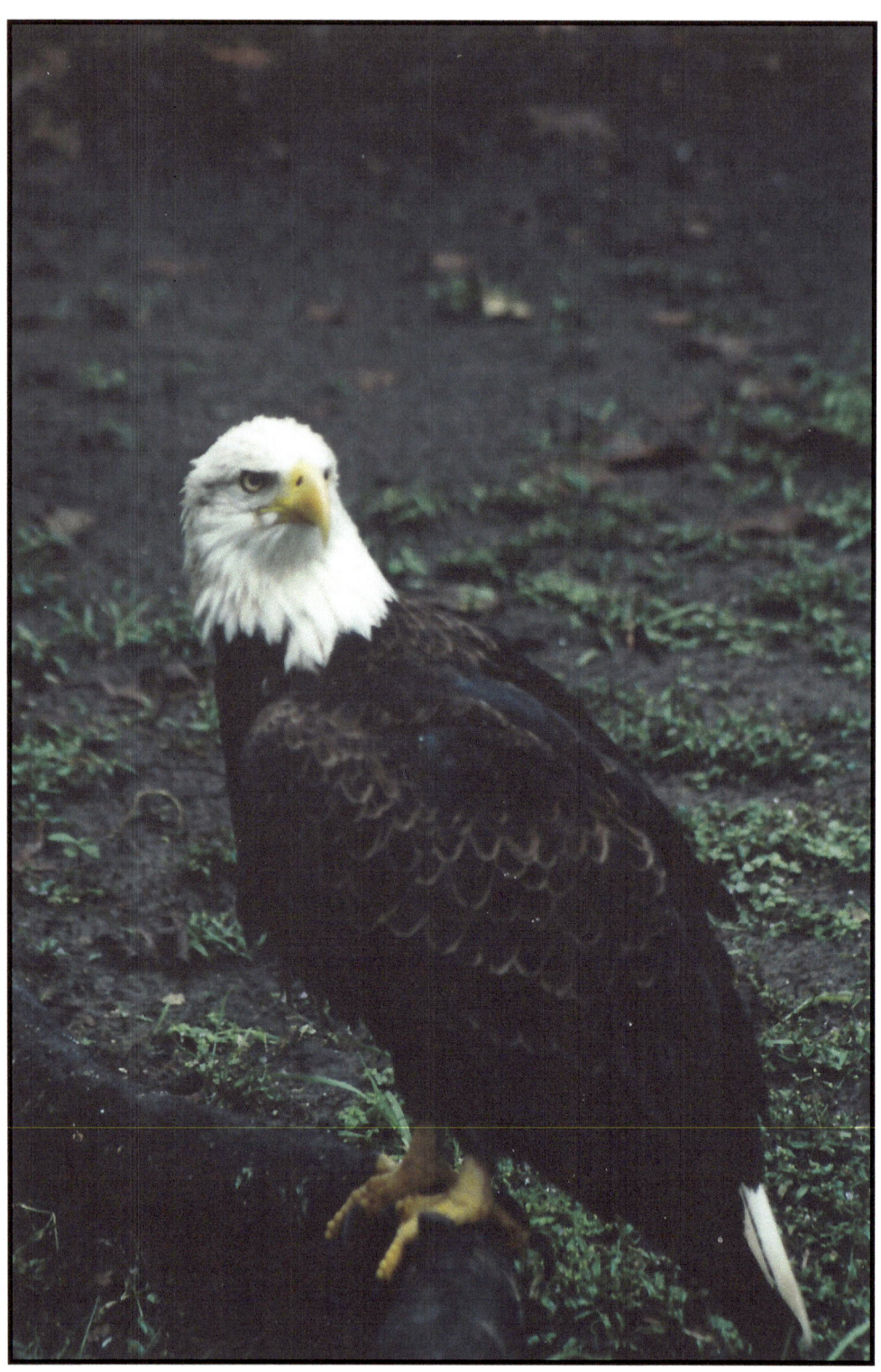

Before embarking on our next photo excursion, I had to decide just how brave I was. Our destination would be the home of several Bald Eagles . However, it was only accessible by boat. Since I can't swim, I wasn't thrilled about our mode of transportation. There were no roads, so all our supplies would have to be packed in boats. Once we began our journey, there would be no turning back.

In the end, the lure of seeing Bald Eagles in the wild, and maybe photographing them, gave me the courage to make the trip.

Just after one in the morning, I heard the familiar sound of a vehicles pulling into the driveway. My fellow adventurers had arrived. Many members of the group had been to our home in the past, but I had to give the newcomers a quick rundown of the house rules.

"Rule number one, the dog's not allowed to have people food. Rule number two, sleep wherever you want, except in my bed. Rule number three, help yourself. If you need something, look for it, and if you can't find it, look some more."

Everyone got settled in rather quickly, so I grabbed the chance to get a few hours of sleep.

Anxious to start our trip, we were up before the sun. After a quick bite to eat, we loaded our gear into the trucks, including my new life jacket, and were on our way.

When we arrived at the river, some of us packed the gear into the boats, while others took the trucks to the location where we would emerge from the river. Jay's mom was there, waiting patiently to drive them back to our starting point. After nearly an hour, the coolers, dry bags, and all our gear were in the boats.

Jay's mom waved to us as the first kayak left the bank of this secluded branch of the Potomac River.

Nervously, I climbed into our canoe, took a deep breath and began paddling. Our group consisted of two canoes, packed with lots of gear, and four kayaks. Floating along in the calm water, we passed an occasional house. Then, we paddled under the old railroad bridge, and left civilization behind.

The river carried us between two mountain ridges. While we floated, a flock of vultures soared high above us in the cloudy sky. The spectacular view of the river and the mountains was breathtaking. I began to relax a little. Water gently lapped against the side of the boat as Jay paddled. A camera in my hands, I sat ready for my first Bald Eagle encounter.

"Put your camera away, there is some rough water ahead," Jay told me.

I realized I could hear the water rushing over the rocks. Quickly, I placed my camera in the spackle bucket, clamped on the lid, and grabbed my paddle.

Suddenly, the water was crashing into the sides of the metal canoe. The impact sounded like thunder. I tried to concentrate on spotting rocks and paddling while water sprayed in my face. Fear gripped me when I heard someone from our group shout, "Stay to the left, it's really nasty on the right!"

Skimming rocks along the way, the canoe lunged from side to side. With my hands tightly gripped to the paddle, I forced myself to stay calm. Finally, we rounded a bend in the river and I could see calmer water ahead. The roar of the water slowly subsided. With a sigh of relief, I spotted the other members of our group as they emptied water from their boats.

Scott waded over, and pulled the front of our canoe up onto the shore. "Now, that wasn't so bad, was it?" He chuckled.

Suddenly, a Bald Eagle swooped down and plucked a fish from the river, not fifty yards in front of us. With his massive wing span, and how swiftly he snatched the fish and was gone, he surprised me.

I had seen my first Bald Eagle in the wild.

As we ventured further down river, Jay proved to be quite good at spotting wildlife. "Bald Eagle to your left, in a tree," he shouted when we rounded a bend.

Quietly, we paddled toward the tree. The eagle slowly turned his head, and glared down at us with his bright yellow eyes. The stark, white, feathers on his head were ruffled by a gentle breeze. My heart was pounding while I zoomed in on him and pushed the shutter button. As we floated past him, I clicked off another frame. He seemed unconcerned by our presence and continued to scan the water for fish.

"Thank you. Hope you catch something," I said.

At first glance, the next portion of the river looked quite treacherous. Then, I realized the water was little more than ankle deep. I listened intently when Jay gave me instructions.

"We are going to get out, and walk alongside the boat. Be careful, the rocks are slippery. The current will carry the boat. When we get to where the guys are, they will help you over the ledge, and I'll get the boat over."

"Ledge? You never told me about a ledge. We're going to do what?" I shrieked.

"Just put your camera away, you'll be fine," he replied.

Soon I was feeling my way along the riverbed, one footstep step at a time. My hands were tightly gripped onto the side of the canoe while we inched our way along.

Suddenly Jay shouted, "Eagle! Get your camera, here he comes."

Within seconds, I let go of the boat, and ripped the lid off the bucket. Framing the eagle's image in the lens, I quickly took the shot. I focused as he flew over my head, and out of sight.

Once again I put my camera away. We weren't far from that dreaded ledge. As we neared it, the current grew stronger and it became more difficult to keep my footing. Just when we reached the ledge, I realized the water plunged over it, and dropped several feet into a deep pool.

Before I knew it, a set of hands was grabbing my arms and pulling me forward. My feet were no longer touching the bottom and I was dropping over the ledge. In an instant, I was under water. The rumbling of the water racing over the rocks was replaced by silence. The gentle breeze that had played with my hair was gone, and there was no air at all. I was rapidly descending into the dark depths of the swift current.

Then, a hand plunged into the water, grabbed my arm, and pulled me upward. Breaking the surface of the water, I gasped for air while Scott pulled me into shallower water.

"I told you this would be fun," he laughed, as I climbed onto the bank. "Relax, you have life jacket on. You would have popped up eventually."

For a moment, I sat to catch my breath while the guys pulled the canoe over the ledge and guided it to the shore. Jay was chatting excitedly about the eagle as he waded over to me. "So, did you get a shot of that eagle before you went swimming?" he asked.

I wasn't amused. After a little encouragement, and assurances that there were no more ledges, I was back in the canoe and we made our way to the campsite.

We set up camp on a ridge about thirty feet above the river. Flash floods were common in this area and we didn't want to take any chances. Past campers had also experienced torrential rains, hail, severe thunderstorms, tornadoes, and, occasionally, warm sunny conditions. Once all our gear was carried up the ridge, we settled in for the night.

I awoke the next morning with Jay shaking me. "Get up! There's an eagle perched right across the river!"

Half asleep, I dressed and gathered my camera equipment. It was barely light out. "Come on. The sun will be up any minute." Jay prodded while I put on my shoes.

Wandering down a narrow deer trail, we made our way through the woods. A gentle breeze drifted in the air, as a few small birds fluttered among the trees. The lush green canopy concealed my view of the eagle until we reached the side of a cliff.

There he sat, proud and strong, perched on an old dead tree. I focused my camera, zoomed in on him, and clicked off a frame. The lighting wasn't very good, but this was a rare opportunity. While I waited for the sun, Jay made his way back to camp. I sat patiently for over a half an hour. Finally, the sun was beginning to glisten through the trees on the mountaintop. A group of crows hollered in the distance.

Then, the eagle spread its wings and took flight. I barely had time to focus the camera before he soared past me, and around the bend in the river.

Some raccoons had visited camp during the night and helped themselves to our breakfast. So we all munched on junk food while we packed up the boats. The sounds of laughter drifted in the air when a few of my fellow campers played in the water.

I stopped to photograph a group of butterflies that had gathered along the water's edge. Their bright yellow and black wings fluttered. The little orange dots that adorned their wings seemed to jump around as they shifted their positions in the sand. Then, the colorful group took flight and drifted away.

We finished packing up our gear, and before long our group was afloat. With my camera in hand, I was a bit more relaxed for the last leg of our journey. Jay had assured me there was only one rough spot ahead of us and it wasn't bad at all.

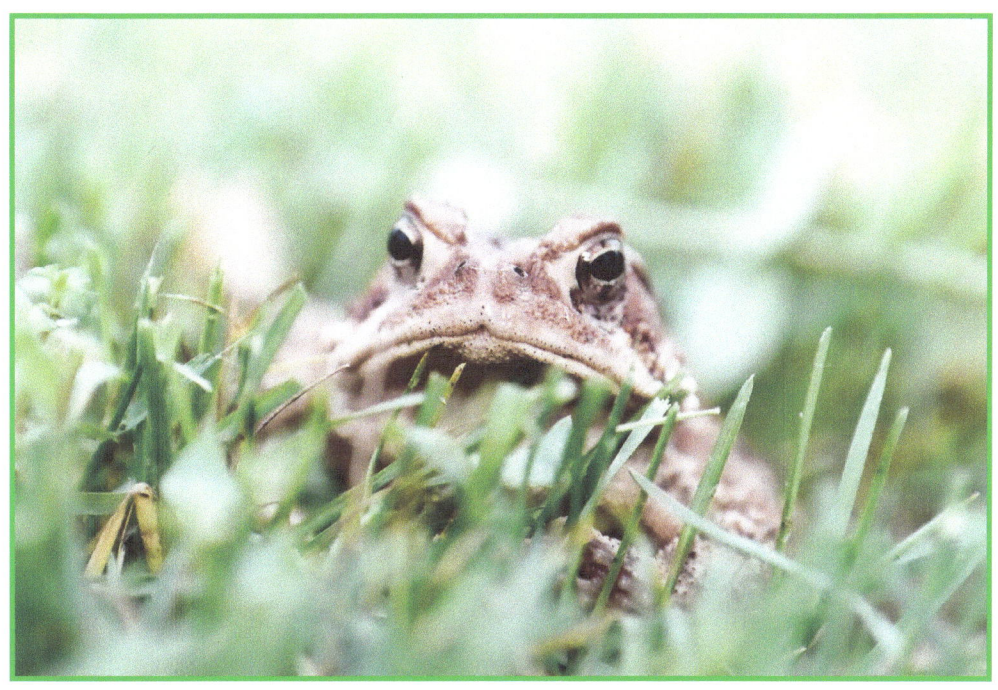

River Excursion

We spent the afternoon drifting along and relaxing. "Osprey straight up, he's got a fish!" Jay shouted.

Just as I focused in the camera, he began shouting again. "Eagles! There's two of them! I bet they go after the Osprey's fish!"

I kept the camera focused on the Osprey and his catch.

Abruptly, the two Bald Eagles came into frame. The Osprey screamed as all three birds collided in midair.

I quickly pushed the shutter button. The lens was filled with feathers and sharp talons.

I tried to stay focused on the fish: that was the prize. Click, click went the camera. Glimpses of white feathers moved in and out of the lens amidst the confusion. The group was slowly drifting downward while they pecked and grabbed at each other.

Just as suddenly as they had appeared, the eagles were gone and so was the fish. I had taken nearly a dozen shots as the scene unfolded.

The hungry, battered Osprey landed on the nearby mountain ridge.

A lone white feather drifted down to the surface of the water.

As our canoe rounded a bend in the river, I could see our vehicles parked along the bank. Less than an hour later, we had packed all our gear back into the trucks.

I stopped for one last shot before heading home.

There, sitting on the bank quietly, observing our group was a lone frog.

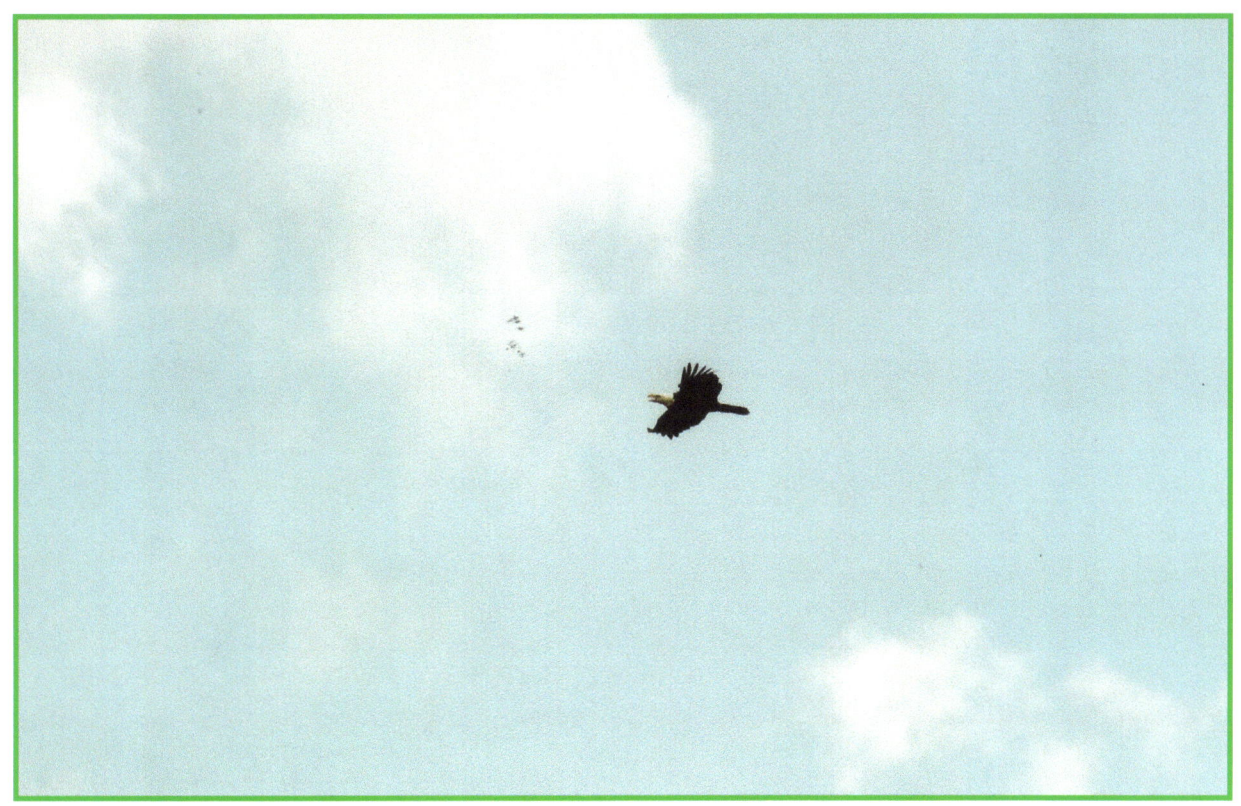

Picturing a Few Birds

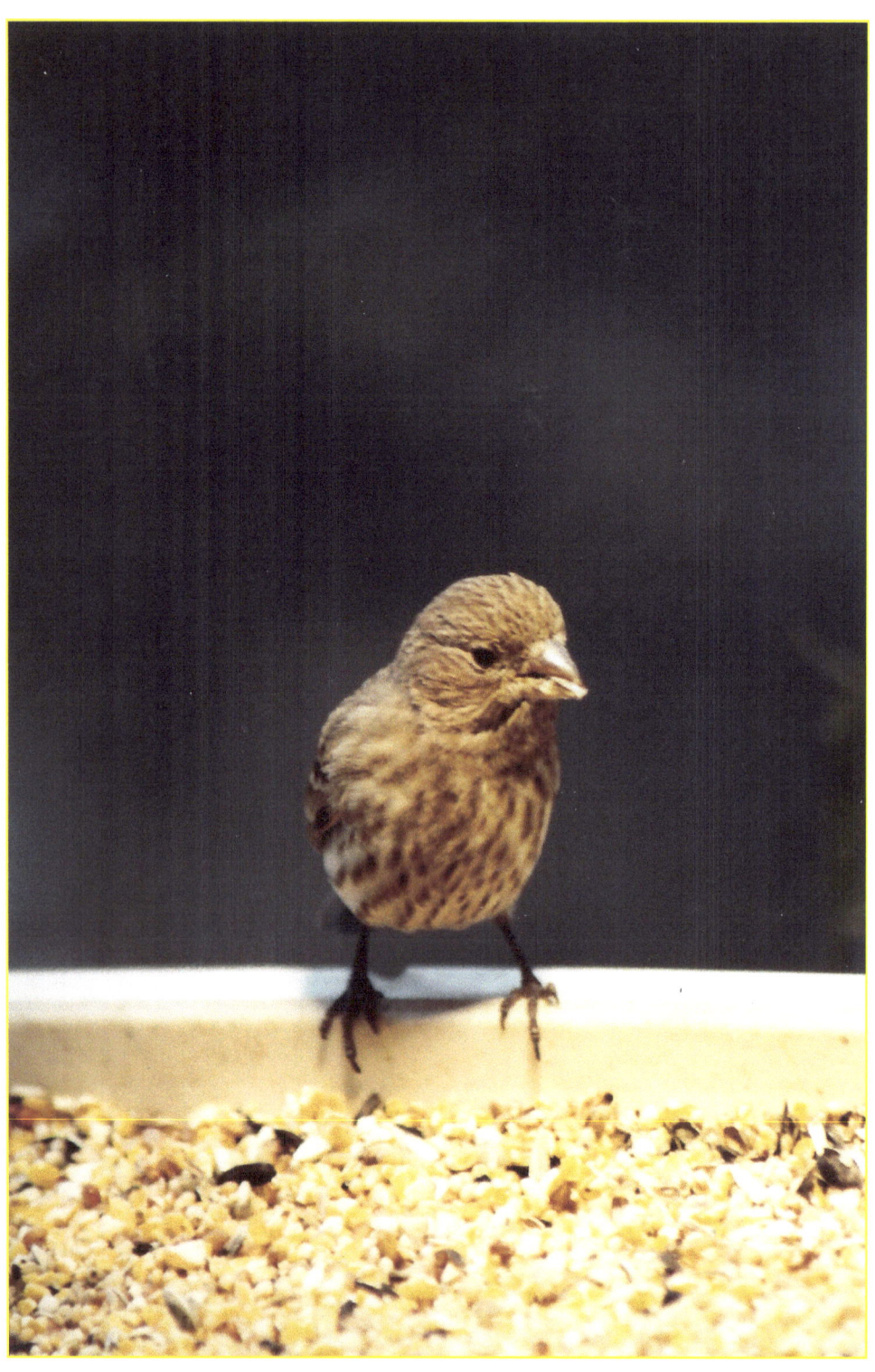

Zack was an energetic four year old who, after an accident, was trapped in a body cast and completely bored. His parents made trip after trip to the library to bring home stacks of books. Each time their choices were rejected. Zack wanted "real" books.

After several long talks with him, they realized he wanted books with photographs not illustrations. So back to the library they went, but came home empty handed. There were no books for his age group with photographs. They then called their favorite wildlife photographer: me.

It seemed like a simple enough request. I only needed to take a group of photographs and construct a story around them. Something to keep Zack interested. I decided to use pictures of birds that Zack could see outside his window. After a few hours of choosing just the right images to build a story around, I hoped for inspiration.

I started with a Robin, a picture of its bright red belly would grab any child's attention. I followed the bird while it searched for a worm to snack on, but a collection of maple leaves cluttering the branch was all I could see. Ducking down, I brought it into focus as it finished off a big, fat, juicy meal. I clicked the shutter button just before he took to the sky. The following image turned out to be a blurry shot of his tail and not the bird in flight hoped for. Eventually, I captured the perfect image.

I turned to a shot of a mockingbird on a wire. This wasn't such an easy shot to get. Since the mockingbird was rather high, I'd also have to get up high without scaring off the bird. Carefully making my way up a sturdy tree across the street from my subject, I centered on the mockingbird with its subtle gray tones, and took the shot before he flew away.

Now I needed to work on the story line. Short sentences would work best for a child of Zack's age; making it rhyme would help the story flow. Soon the story line took shape. The reader could take a walk and see a variety of birds along the way.

Next, I added in a chickadee with its tiny pointed beak as it chirped happily on a branch. Its soft melody carried through the afternoon air when I captured it on film. With the addition of a bright red cardinal and red winged blackbird, I was making progress.

I lay on the ground to get the photograph of a dove to add to the story. I moved closer and took another shot. I moved closer still. The bird's delicate feathers filled the frame with a multitude of gray shades as its pitch black eye watched me.

Seeing birds is relatively easy; photographing them isn't. This dove made things quite easy and later that same day peeked in my kitchen window. That's when I took the photo that ended up as the back cover of the book.

I decided not to include the hummingbird picture so the book wouldn't be too long. The hummingbird's sword-like beak dwarfed his tiny face. The collection of delicate feathers covering his body shimmered in the afternoon sun when I captured him on film. Looking at the photograph, I recalled the subtle humming sound the bird's wings made while it hovered above the bright red feeder.

Picturing A Few Birds

A woodpecker made me work to get its picture. Spotting it in a tree at the park, it seemed as soon as I thought about taking its picture, the woodpecker would dart to another tree. I watched and waited until he was busy gorging himself on bugs before trying to approach him again, only to have him dash off to another tree. Finally, I spotted him on the trunk of a nearby tree. Quickly, I snapped the picture and hoped it would be a good image.

Once the story and the photographs were coordinated, the photos were scanned onto my computer, the text was added, and then the whole thing was printed. After stapling the pages together I took the book to Zack.

I sat on the edge of the couch as he and I read the book together.

It was a hit. Zack showed his new book to everyone who came to visit him.

Soon I was getting phone calls from the parents of Zack's friends; they wanted copies of the book for their own children. This prompted me to try my luck at selling them. I enlisted the help of a local writer who taught me about copyrights, ISBN numbers, and editing. After a few of subtle changes, I sent copies to friends with small children and asked them to let me know what they and their children thought.

Before long I added the book to my website, and took it along to exhibits and lectures. Soon I began getting phone calls from parents asking me to produce a second book. They were tired of reading the same book night after night.

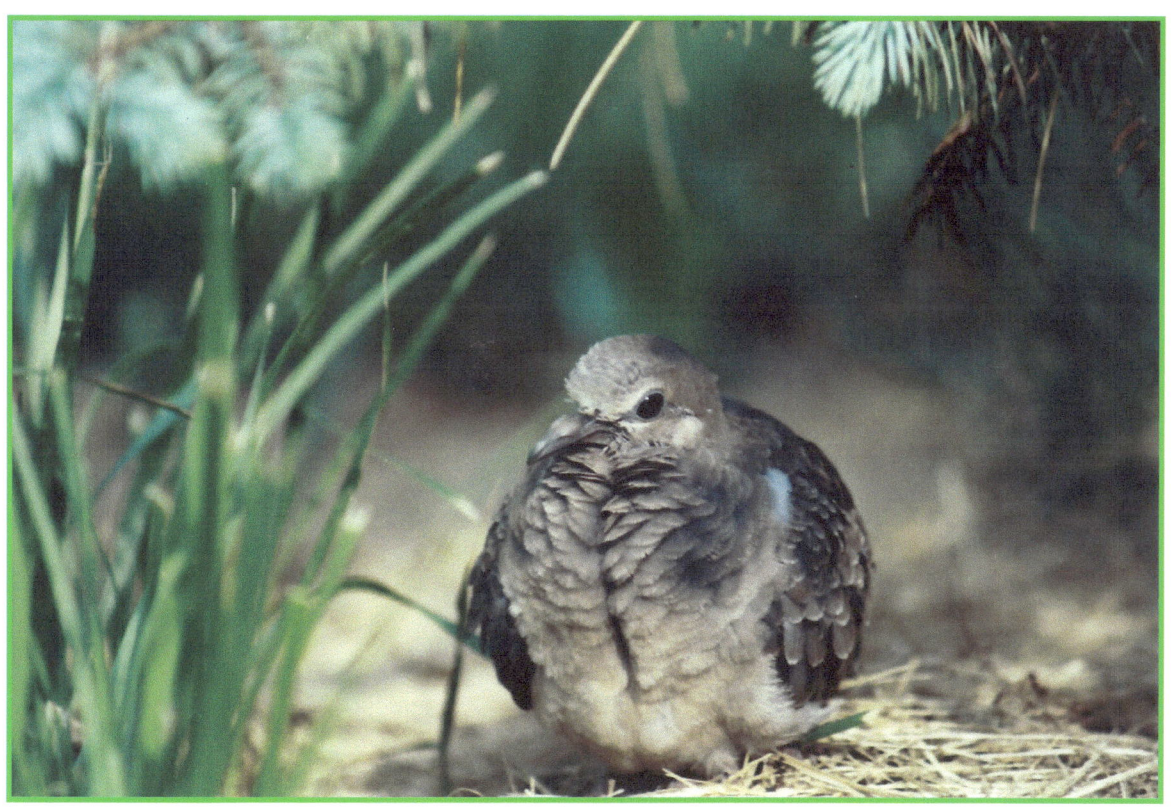

Lost

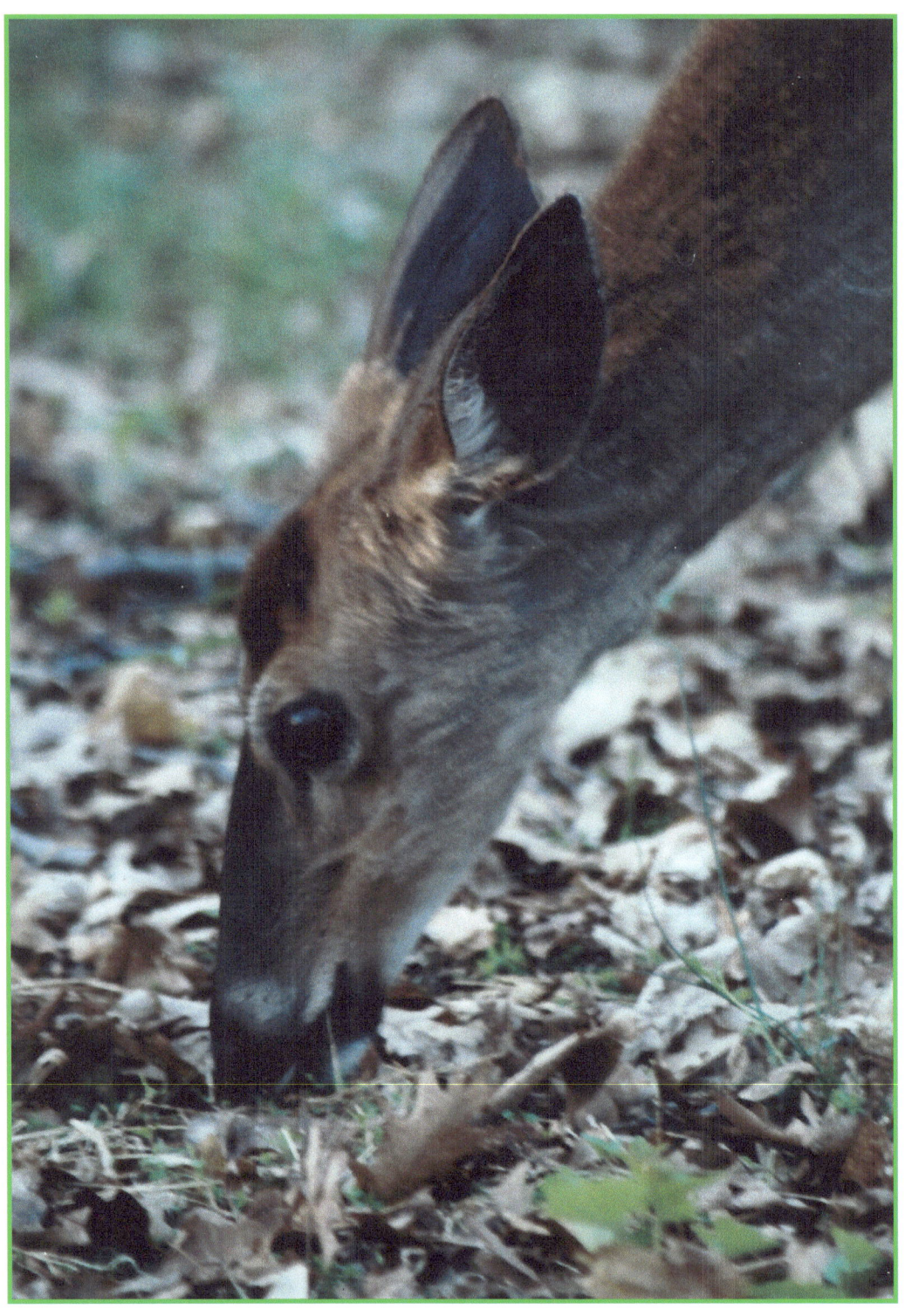

Rattling and groaning from time to time, our old truck twisted and turned along the narrow mountain road. The landscape seemed to be an endless series of hills and valleys. Hundreds of large sturdy trees covered the area and lined the narrow roadway that seemed to meander on for miles. In the distance, I could hear the carefree calls from a variety of songbirds.

I was elated when a lone deer wandered onto the road a few feet in front of the truck. Through the windshield, I focused my camera and snapped a quick photo. When I exited the truck, the crisp mountain air engulfed me. As I stepped closer to the doe, I noticed she had a few friends hiding in the trees, and my excitement grew. I focused in on the deer in the road. Her ears twitched as I slowly depressed the shutter button. I was sure this would produce a blurry shot. I quickly clicked off one more shot before the frightened doe hurried off to join her friends. Almost instantly, the herd disappeared into the thick underbrush at the edge of the woods.

We proceeded further into the park. Jay spotted an enormous red tailed hawk on the ground. It had just caught a meal.

We quietly got out and approached the raptor. His attention was focused on his meal. The bright white feathers of his underbelly helped me focus in on him while we ventured further into the woods.

With a sudden flap of his wings, he flew off with his coveted squirrel dinner dangling from his claws. The weight of his catch prevented him from flying above the tree tops. I made my way through the woods while trying to keep the hawk in sight. The rough terrain worked to the hawk's advantage and soon he was out of sight.

As we walked back to the truck in the distance, I heard an odd sound. Jay and I both stopped and looked at each other.

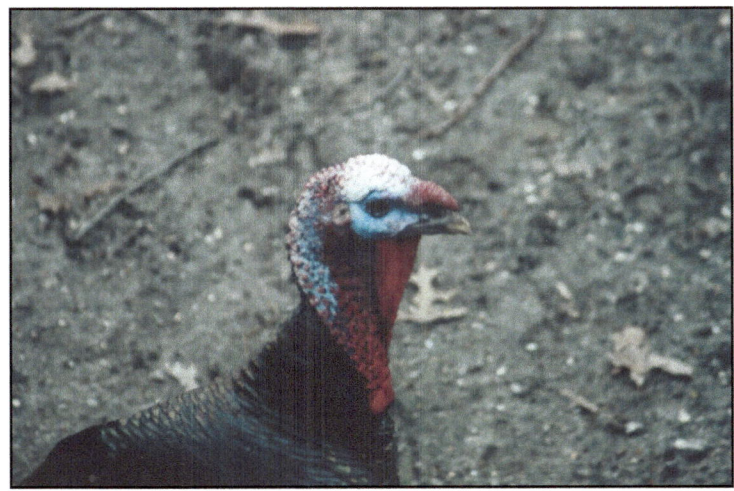

"What was that?" I whispered.

"A turkey maybe, go see. I'll wait here." Jay whispered.

So I proceeded toward the sound. The area was speckled with rock ledges, thick underbrush, and old trees.

Through the woods I trekked while peering around one tree after another in hopes of spotting the turkey. My plan was to focus in on its bright red wattle. Perhaps I could find the illusive turkey as it was joined by other turkeys. This would give me the opportunity to photograph the entire flock.

Lost

After hiking up over an embankment, I stopped to listen. All I heard was silence, not a single gobble or twig snapping anywhere.

When I turned around, I realized I had lost sight of Jay and the roadway. I was further into the woods than I thought.

Suddenly, I heard the turkey gobble once again, there off to my right. My attention was refocused on my goal: a photograph of a wild turkey.

Climbing over a very large log and through some brush, I heard him again. He was closer now. I began climbing up yet another embankment. I was using the branches of a bush to pull myself up over the top.

Then, I found myself face to face with a large buck. He was peering over the edge of the hill—staring straight down at me.

We were literally a few feet apart.

I managed to get both feet planted firmly on the ground with very little movement. He snorted at me as I repositioned myself.

"Hello, I'm just going to get a quick picture, and then I'll leave you alone."

I slowly and carefully positioned the camera and touched the shutter button while he studied me.

"Damn, it's not turned on."

The deer was gone.

I climbed up to the top of the hill where he had stood. Looking around I had hoped to spot him nearby. There was no sign of the deer or the turkey.

"Thanks anyway."

I decided I should make my way back to the truck. However, while I was busy following the turkey, I hadn't paid much attention to where I was going. I gazed back down the hill and nothing looked familiar. I remembered climbing over a large log but it was nowhere in sight.

I was lost.

I wondered if I should stay put, or try to find my way back. After a few minutes, I decided to look for the road. I began descending through the trees. Soon I was brushing branches out of my way and climbing over rocks. I sat down and listened, hoping Jay was calling me. All I heard was silence.

As I emerged over the top of a ridge the glare from the setting sun blinded me.

I trampled through brush and over several downed trees. I walked around the sturdy oaks that broke up the evening sky. Suddenly, there was movement in the distance.

Was it Jay?

No, it was the turkey. He was standing there looking around and calling to his fellow fowl.

Re-energized, I quickly snapped a picture and inched closer. Peering through the lens, I clicked the shutter button once more. More confident now, I crawled forward to get another shot, but the turkey quickly fled.

I had found the turkey, had a close encounter with a deer, but I was still lost.

I lost my footing and fell to the ground. There I sat in the middle of a bush scratched and disheartened. Darkness was slowly encompassing me. As I was brushing myself off I noticed the road below. After what seemed like an eternity, I stepped out of the woods and onto the rough hard surface.

Looking around I realized the truck could be miles away from here.

As I wandered down the road, I heard rustling in the brush up on the hill. It was almost completely dark out now. I knew there was something there, but I couldn't make out what it was. I headed toward the sounds. I was sure it was probably another deer or turkey. Then I saw a light among the trees; it was someone with a flashlight. I wasn't alone after all. Suddenly, a beam of light blinded me.

"What are you doing over there?"

With a sigh of relief, I answered, "Jay?"

As I walked toward the light, I composed myself and tried to hide my excitement.

"Oh, I'm just wandering around, looking for critters to photograph. What are you doing up there?"

"Looking for you, where have you been?"

"Sorry, I took the scenic route. While I was looking for the turkey I ran into a deer. Then on my way back I found the turkey."

I decided not to tell Jay just how lost I was. After all, everything turned out okay.

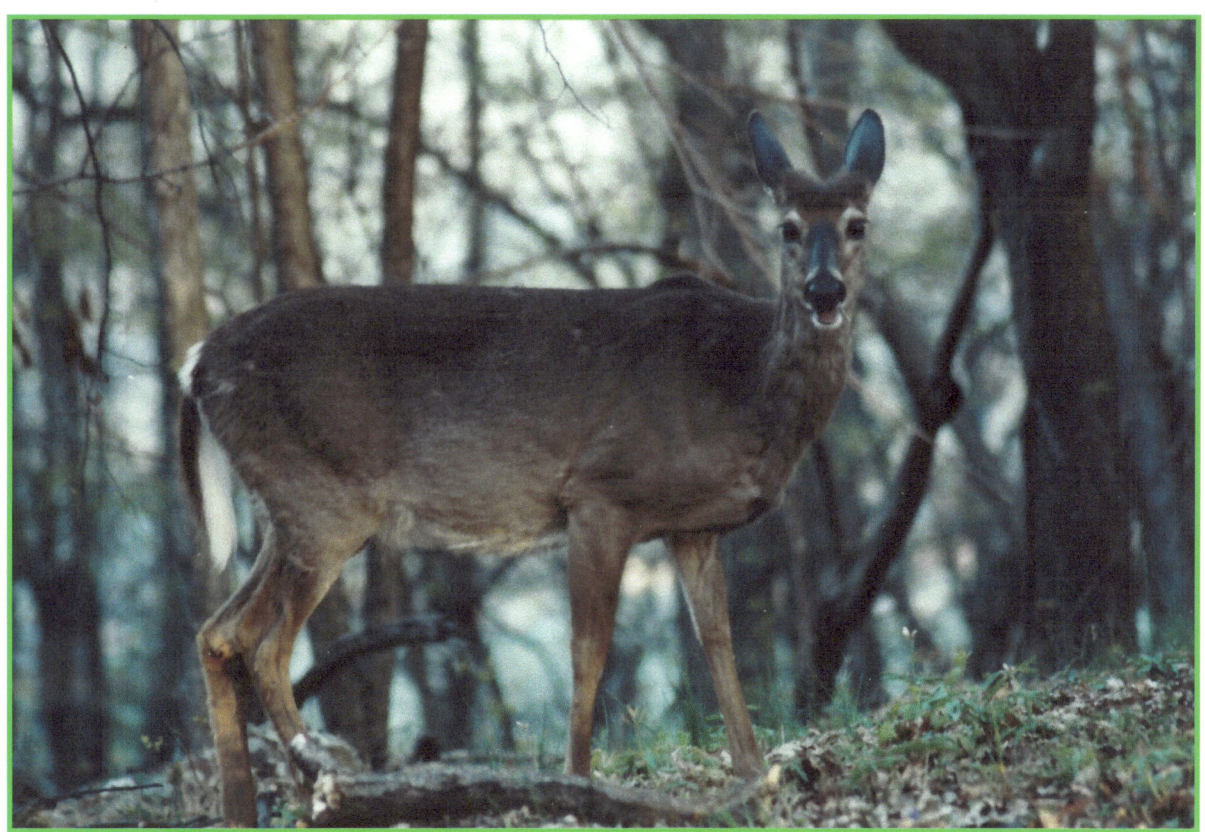

Northern Expedition

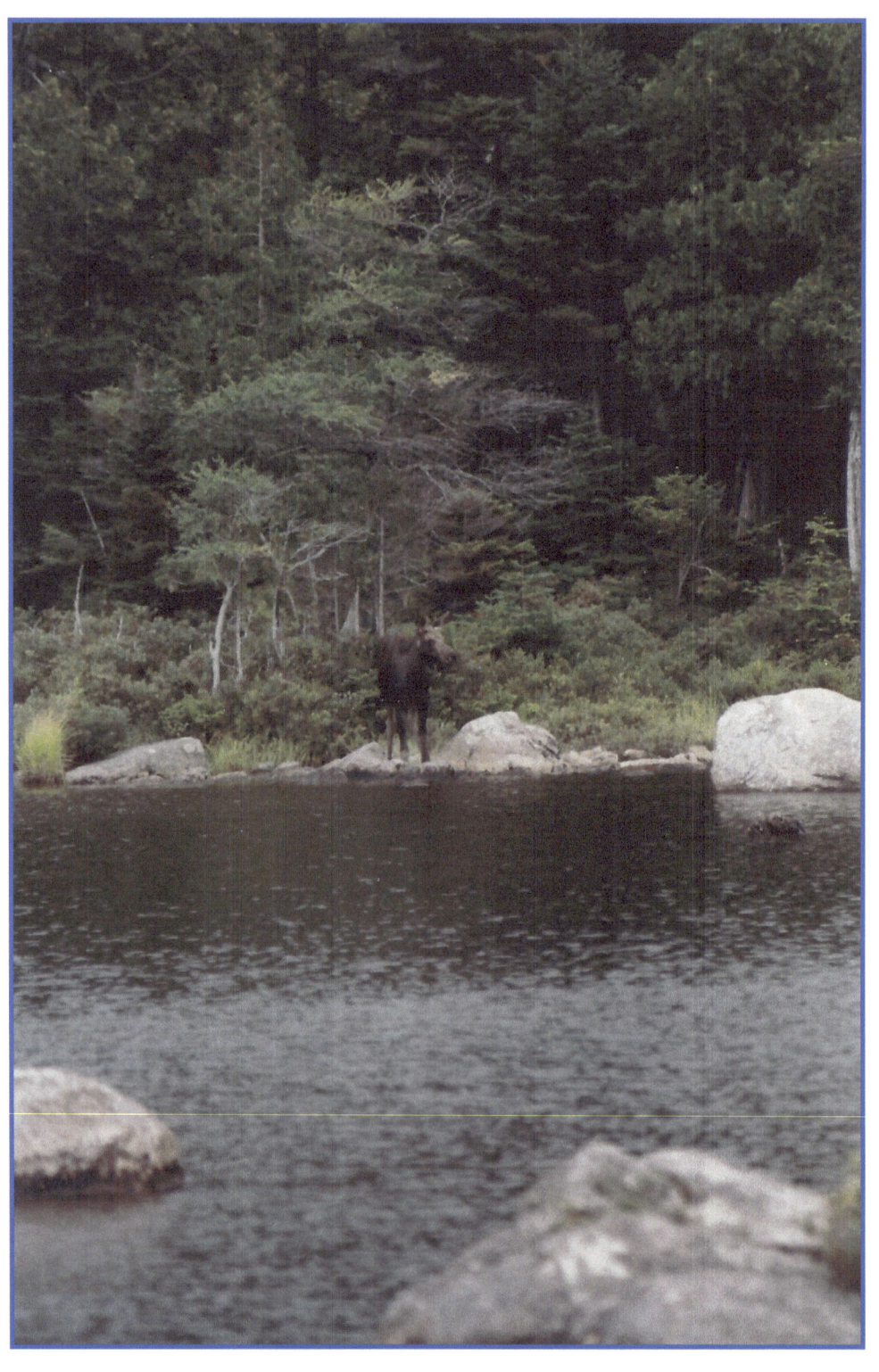

Jay and I traveled all the way to Maine just to photograph moose.

After days of looking, we still hadn't found one. On day four, we explored more of the countryside before stopping for breakfast. At a small diner, we talked with a few local residents. They all agreed we needed to visit the reverse waterfall nearby.

After driving around on back roads for nearly an hour, we knew we were lost. Then Jay spotted a crudely made sign:

"Directions to reverse waterfall: 25 cents."

What luck. Out here, in the middle of nowhere, we found directions. Curious, I got out of the truck and wandered over to the sign. Beneath it was a small wooden box. Inside were several copies of a map and four quarters. I added a quarter to the box, and retrieved a map.

After studying the paper for a few minutes, we found our way to the falls.

Wandering along the water's edge, Jay noticed something in the distance.

At first glance it appeared to be a rock, but it was moving against the current. Slowly, the form moved closer. It was a seal. We watched it playfully swim about for a few minutes before he swam around a bend.

Hiking along a narrow path and up a hillside, we cleared the trees and found ourselves on a small cliff.

A number of seals were in the water below. One by one, they swam against the current, diving headfirst into the water. Their slick, gray bodies surfaced then submerged again. The joyful barks of the seals echoed through the valley while I finished off a roll of film.

In an effort to get a little closer, we began our decent. Inch by inch, we scaled rocks, climbed around brush, and eventually reached the water's edge. Patiently, I sat watching and waiting for one of the seals to come closer.

Little by little, the seals were drifting our way.

One lone seal decided to be brave and investigate the strangers.

Sitting on the ground, I leaned out over the water and zoomed in when his head broke the surface of the water. He turned around and dove back in while I was adjusting the focus on the camera. A minute later, his dark, wet head emerged once again.

"Smile," I prompted.

Inching closer, he reminded me of a curious child when he looked into the lens. I held down the shutter button as large drops of water streamed from his face. In one swift motion, he turned and with a splash, was gone. He resurfaced in the middle of the group of seals. Together, they made their way out of the cove and downriver.

The tide was coming in. Water rushed up and over the rocks to create the reverse waterfall we had come to see. The roar of the water drowned out the songs of the nearby birds. The rushing tide forced the water level to rise and swallow up the smaller rocks. Little by little, the incline along the bank disappeared as the river widened its berth.

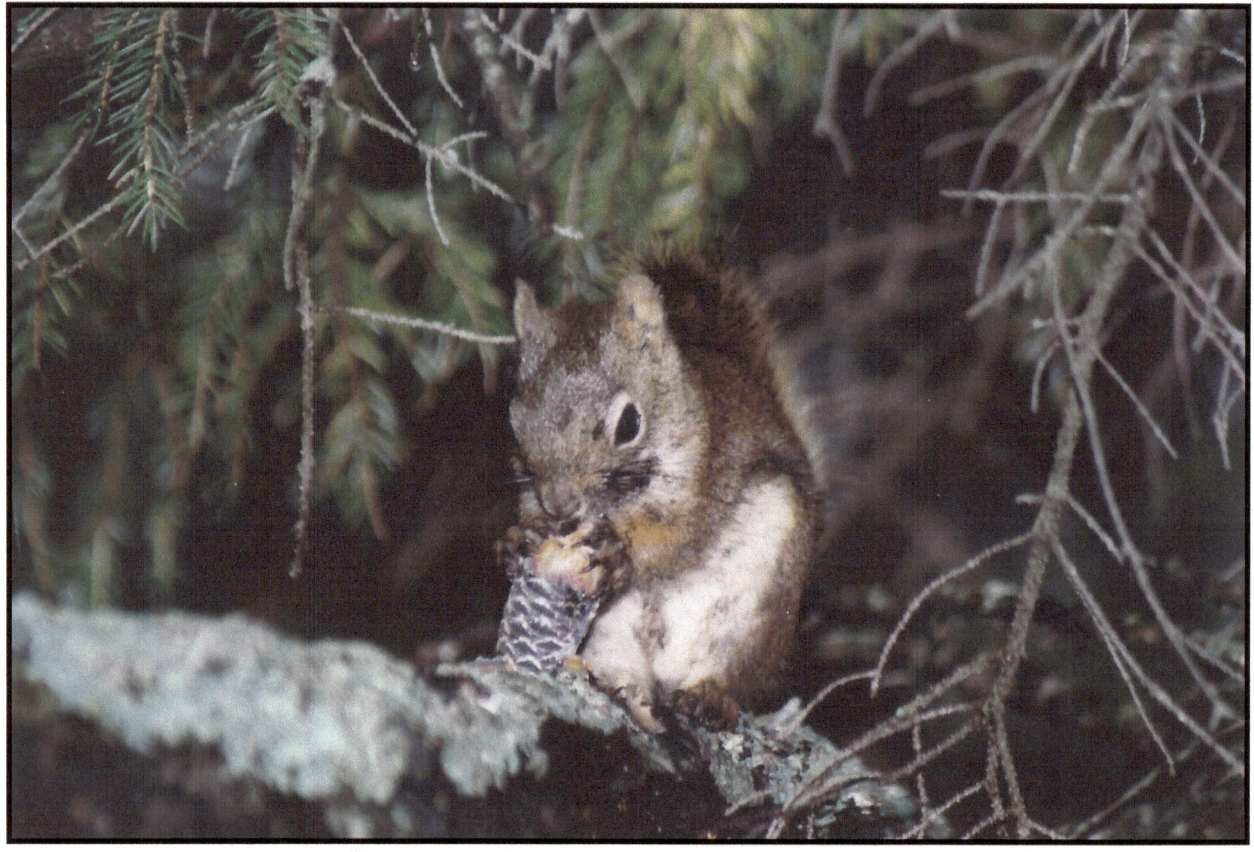

We made our way back up the steep incline to get a better view. A large object bobbed in the water. With a thud, an empty rowboat crashed into the rocks as it made its way around the bend and out of sight. Wondering where it would end its journey, we listened to it hit more rocks further downriver.

It was time to head back to our hotel to look over some maps and notes, before embarking on our search that evening.

Right before sunset, we checked a few locations local residents had directed us to in our quest for a moose. After several hours, we opted to give up the search and get some dinner. During our meal, it was decided that in the morning we would head for the Great North Woods. Over dessert, we looked over our collection of maps and planned out our route. We guessed it would be about a three-hour drive further north.

The buzzing of the alarm clock woke us at 4 am. After loading up the camera equipment, maps, and snacks, we drove onto the empty highway. Venturing down one dark deserted road after another, we watched for wildlife. We were both hoping to spot a moose, but a deer, fox, or even opossum would do.

As daylight emerged, we arrived at our destination. Our hearts sank when we drove into an area reserved for parking. The slamming of car doors and happy conversation drifted in the gentle breeze. There were dozens of hikers everywhere. Scattered into small groups, they were putting on their backpacks, lacing up their boots and collecting their supplies.

The chances of spotting a moose with all these people around seemed pretty slim. However, the Great North Woods stretched for miles. There were a variety of trees, lakes, meadows, and some very large mountains.

Maybe we would get lucky. Stopping at the check in station, we were informed that most of the hikers were headed up and over the mountains. So we signed in, studied a map of the area, and headed down a narrow trail.

Crossing over rustic wooden bridges and weaving our way through the woods, we encountered a red squirrel. He sat perched on a branch, quietly nibbling at a pine cone as I approached. He seemed unconcerned by my presence when I framed him in the lens. Nervously, I gently stepped even closer and zoomed in on his tiny features.

His delicate looking reddish brown paws gripped the meal. He worked at the cone with his small sharp teeth, while I ventured even closer. The squirrel's pitch black eyes glanced from side to side while I depressed the shutter button. When he stopped eating and turned all his attention to me, I decided to back away and let him eat in peace.

"Thank you. Enjoy your breakfast."

We proceeded along the trail until we emerged from the woods along the shore of a lake. Stopping for a moment, we scanned the shoreline for any signs of movement.

While we took in the view, a mother moose and her calf wandered out of the woods. I was amazed at how large they both were. Through the trees, we watched her lead her calf to the water's edge. The mother moose prodded her baby with her long square nose as they walked among the rocks and ventured into the water. As she waded out further and further, Mom called to her baby, who nervously followed.

Water cascaded off their deep brown coats as they proceeded through the water. Slowly, they crossed in front of us.

Just as I finished off a roll of film, it began to rain. I quickly put in a new roll of film and pulled out a poncho. It had taken us days to find these two; I wasn't going to let a little rain deter me.

The pair had paused in front of us. I was trying to remain quiet and move as little as possible, but I knew that they were aware of our presence. I decided to take a chance and see if I could get just a little closer. Slowly, I inched my way along a boulder that protruded out into the water. I lay on the jagged surface and found the pair in the lens.

As I focused in on them, the calf began to wander away from Mom and back to the shore. The large cow didn't seem concerned, and began to graze on the long grass that grew in the shallow water. I was surprised at how far the youngster roamed.

The rain subsiding, I climbed around the rock to get pictures from different angles. The mother moose would totally immerse her head in the water. After grabbing a mouthful of grass, she would pop her head up. As the water rolled off her head, I zoomed in and took a few shots. Large drops of water ran down her ears and face while I clicked off frame after frame. The sun was slowly emerging from the clouds to reflect in her wet coat. Every few minutes, she would scan the area to locate her calf.

After nearly an hour, the mother moose made her way to the shore to reunite with her calf. The pair then proceeded back out into the water and made their way across the lake.

Jay and I watched them emerge on the opposite shore. Shaking the water from their coats, they both glanced in our direction before making their way into the trees and out of sight.

TO THE RESCUE

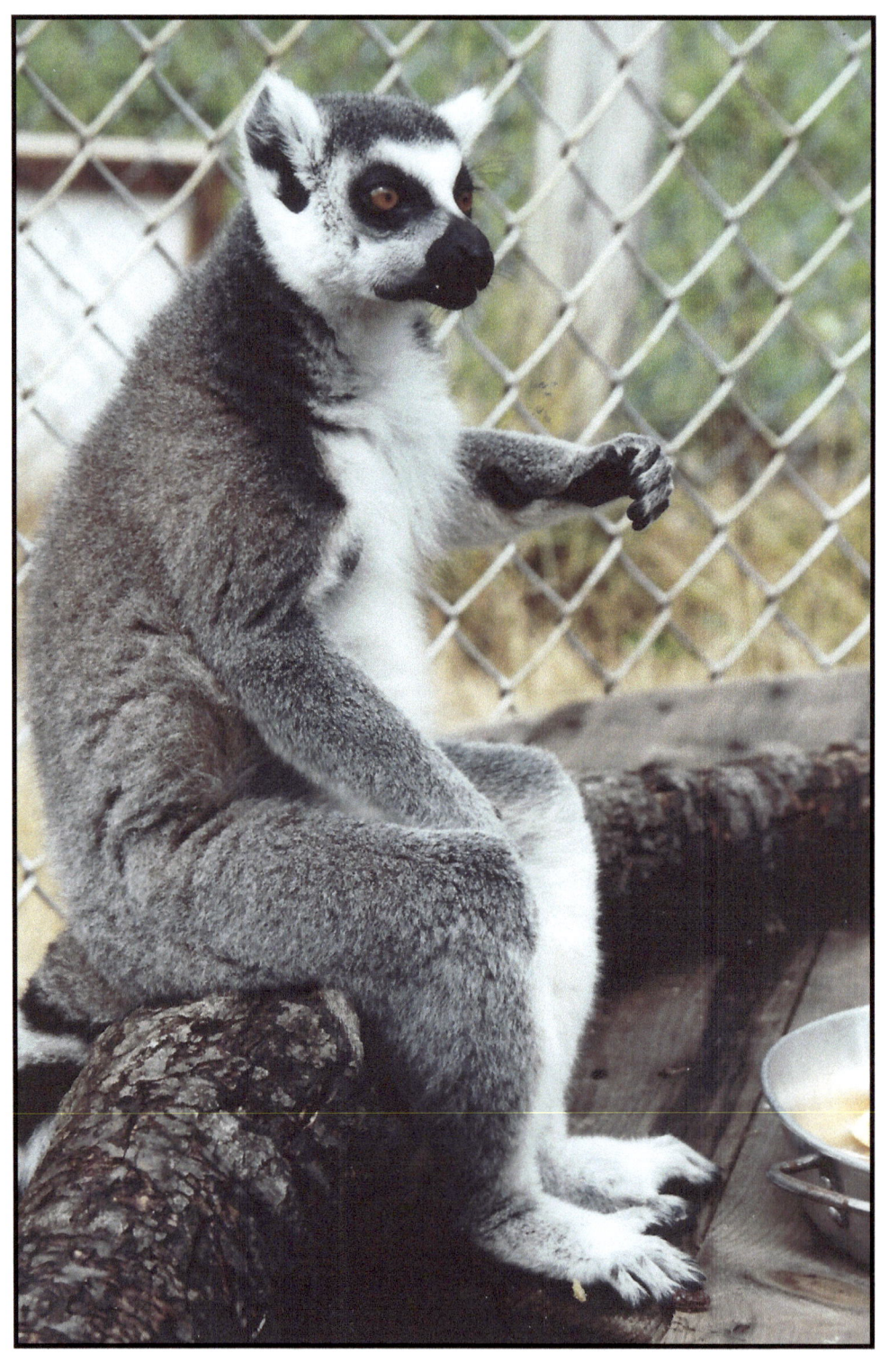

While I always prefer photographing animals in the wild, occasionally I take advantage of the photo opportunities offered by zoos and rescue facilities that care for captive wild animals.

At one such location, they housed animals that had once been considered exotic pets. Most were cute and appealing when they were young, but soon outgrew their appeal. In addition, there were a few wild animals from the area that couldn't survive on their own.

I had been invited to photograph the animals for a project the owners were working on. Harry was a tall, thin man with wavy, dark hair. His hands were callused and scratched from years of hard work. Sally was a thin, short woman with muscular arms. When we arrived, she was bottle-feeding a fawn while we spoke.

Jay and I had packed the truck with food for the animals. We knew this was a shoestring operation, and donations played a major part in keeping it running.

As with most zoos and parks of this kind, there was a barrier or extra row of fencing to keep the public and animals separate. This was in addition to the enclosures that the animals lived it. We were going beyond that extra barrier and right up to, or in some cases, into the cages.

Harry escorted us to the back part of the park. From there, we could access all the animals.

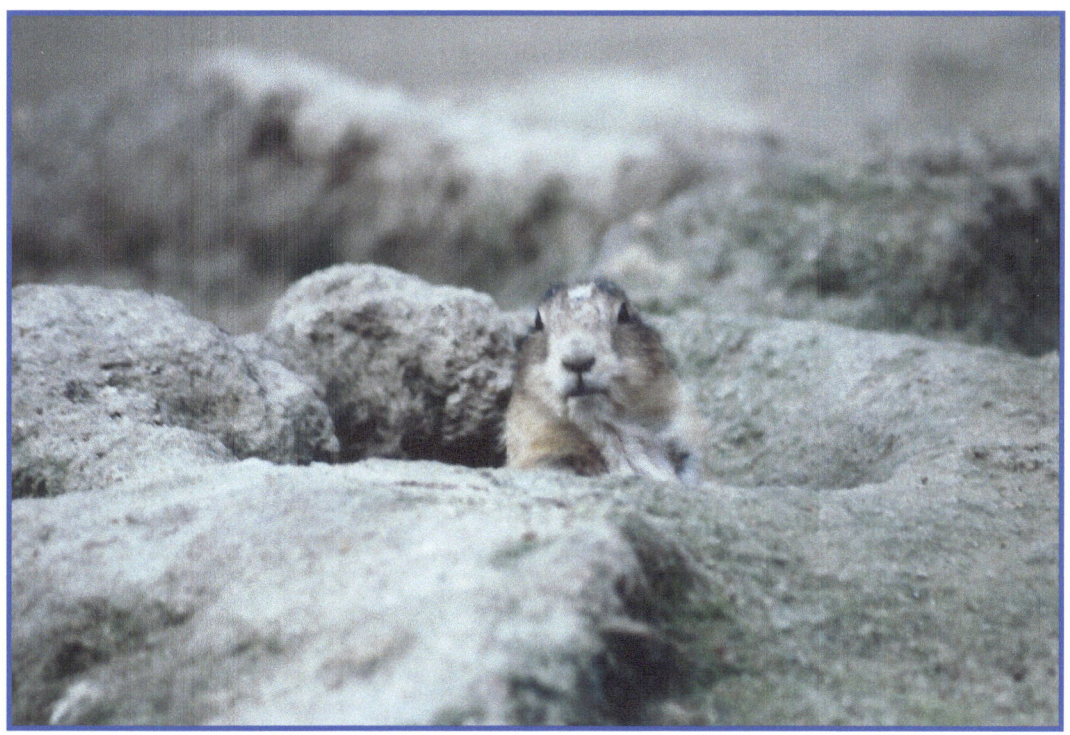

To the Rescue

Before long, Jay was tossing pieces of chicken to the alligator while I was clicking the shutter button. The alligator's thick hide made him seem quite slow and cumbersome; however, he showed us just how quick he was when he jumped to catch a chicken leg. Changing the angle of the camera, I took a profile shot of him, and then I clicked the shutter button just as he opened wide to show off his razor sharp teeth. He had a sinister-looking smile as his powerful jaws clamped down on the meal.

The bears enjoyed the berries and dog food we brought them. They seemed to like having their pictures taken. As I zoomed in on one of the bears, his sorrowful looking eyes gazed right into the lens. While the other bear splashed about in the moat, the bright morning sun danced on his wet coat. Large drops of water fell from his thick black fur when I captured him on film.

Then it was on to the prairie dogs. They proved to be a challenge; several of them were poking their heads out of their burrows. When I approached them, they would all run underground. So I had to sit and wait them out.

"Peak-a-boo. Gotcha, gotcha again. Thanks guys."

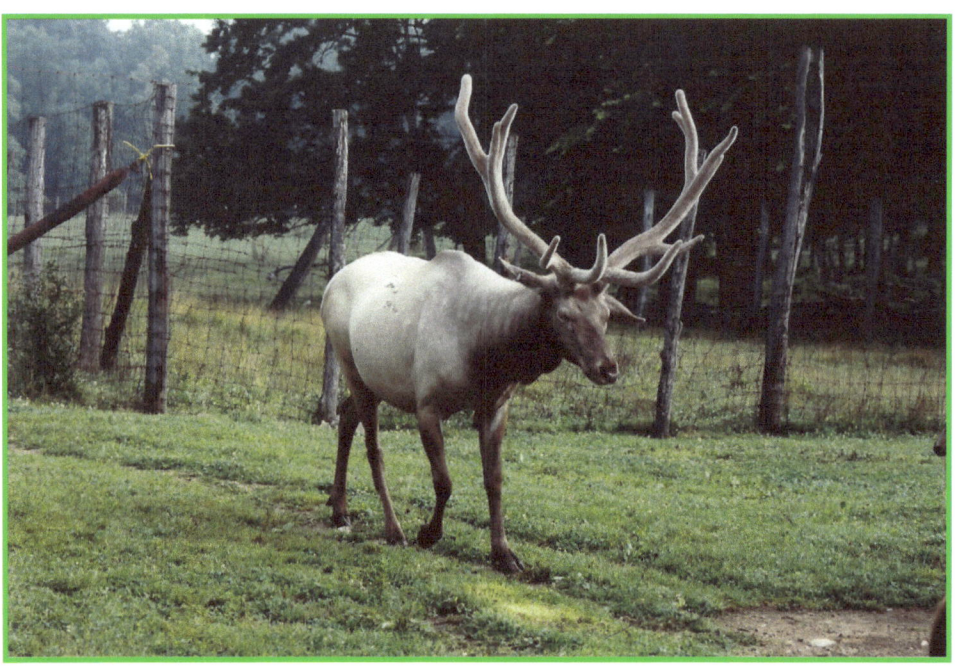

When it was time to feed the elk, Harry stood by the fence and shook the feed bucket. An entire herd of elk suddenly appeared from a wooded area. One by one, they wandered to the feed trough for their breakfast. Placing my camera on the fencing, I snapped picture after picture.

Right when I zoomed out to get a shot of the entire herd, Harry exclaimed, "Here comes Elvis!"

Elvis, the only adult male in the group, was enormous. His feet pounded the ground when he walked. His shiny, tan coat seemed to glisten in the morning sun, reflecting an array of different shades. His thick, powerful neck supported his huge head which was topped off by the largest set of antlers I had ever seen. He was so big that I had trouble getting all of him in the lens. I stopped to marvel at his size. This gentle giant slowly made his way through the herd. When his head bumped the fencing, the entire fence shook. He stopped for a moment and observed me.

"Go ahead, rub his nose he likes that," Harry instructed.

Nervously, I put my hand through the fence and rubbed his sleek, soft fur. He studied me with his large, black eyes. I was amazed that such a powerful creature could be so gentle. All too soon, it was time to move on and feed the other animals.

In the barn, I photographed a group of ostriches; this was a bit tricky. One of them was determined to peck at the lens of the camera. After several attempts, I realized that he would stomp his foot immediately before trying to attack the camera. So I had Jay watch his foot while I zoomed in on his face. I successfully framed his head and neck in the lens. I refocused the camera and blurred the background. The result was a beautiful vertical portrait.

The lynx was quite cooperative. Harry distracted her to the other end of the cage. Then I began talking to her. She approached as the camera clicked off shot after shot. I pointed the lens at the stark black lines that accented her face. Her ears twitched while she posed for me. But I don't think she enjoyed having her picture taken at all. After a few minutes, she hissed and showed me her teeth. She had had enough. It was time to move on.

After some brief instructions, I was in the enclosure with the lemurs.

This was a real thrill.

These docile, gentle creatures were a bit leery of me. I made sure I moved slowly so that I wouldn't frighten them. At first, they kept their distance; this allowed me to get a picture of the group gathered together.

Eventually, one of them came over to investigate me. He reached out with his tiny paw and touched me. I remained motionless and let him get comfortable with my presence. He seemed to be examining me with his round orange eyes. Slowly, I began to move and raise the camera to my face. Looking through the lens, I could see him staring back at me.

"Hello," I whispered softly.

Stark white fur began on his face, and proceeded to cover his entire underside. His back was covered with thick short fur in various shades of gray. He studied me for a moment. I took the opportunity to get another photograph of him. This time, I managed to get all of him in the shot, even his long ringed tail.

The others seemed less concerned with my presence. I zoomed in on them while they happily munched on bananas and berries. To me, each of these encounters was a special moment in my life, and was over far too soon.

I was placed in the cage with some enormous iguanas. I didn't realize they could get that large. One of them was gripped to the side of the enclosure by his sharp claws. He seemed to be smiling at me. I am not a big fan of reptiles, so I didn't spend much time with them. But I did get some really nice close-up shots of their faces.

An array of parrots were housed here; most had simply outlived their owners or their appeal. As I focused in one bird after another, I noticed each had its own unique personality.

There was an African Gray parrot with a mischievous look in his eyes. Delicate feathers in subtle shades from white to dark gray covered his body. He shook his deep red tail feathers as I zoomed in for a photograph. Beside him was a bright white cockatoo. He was squawking loudly while I framed in his dark black beak. I took a moment to get a vertical shot of him. I wanted to capture all of him on film including the sharp talons that gripped the perch.

We discovered the llamas were quite friendly, and curious about the camera. If Jay distracted them a little, I could get pictures from a few different angles instead of simply close ups of their noses.

By day's end, I had hundreds of photographs to add to my portfolio, as well as memories that would last me a lifetime.

Going Solo

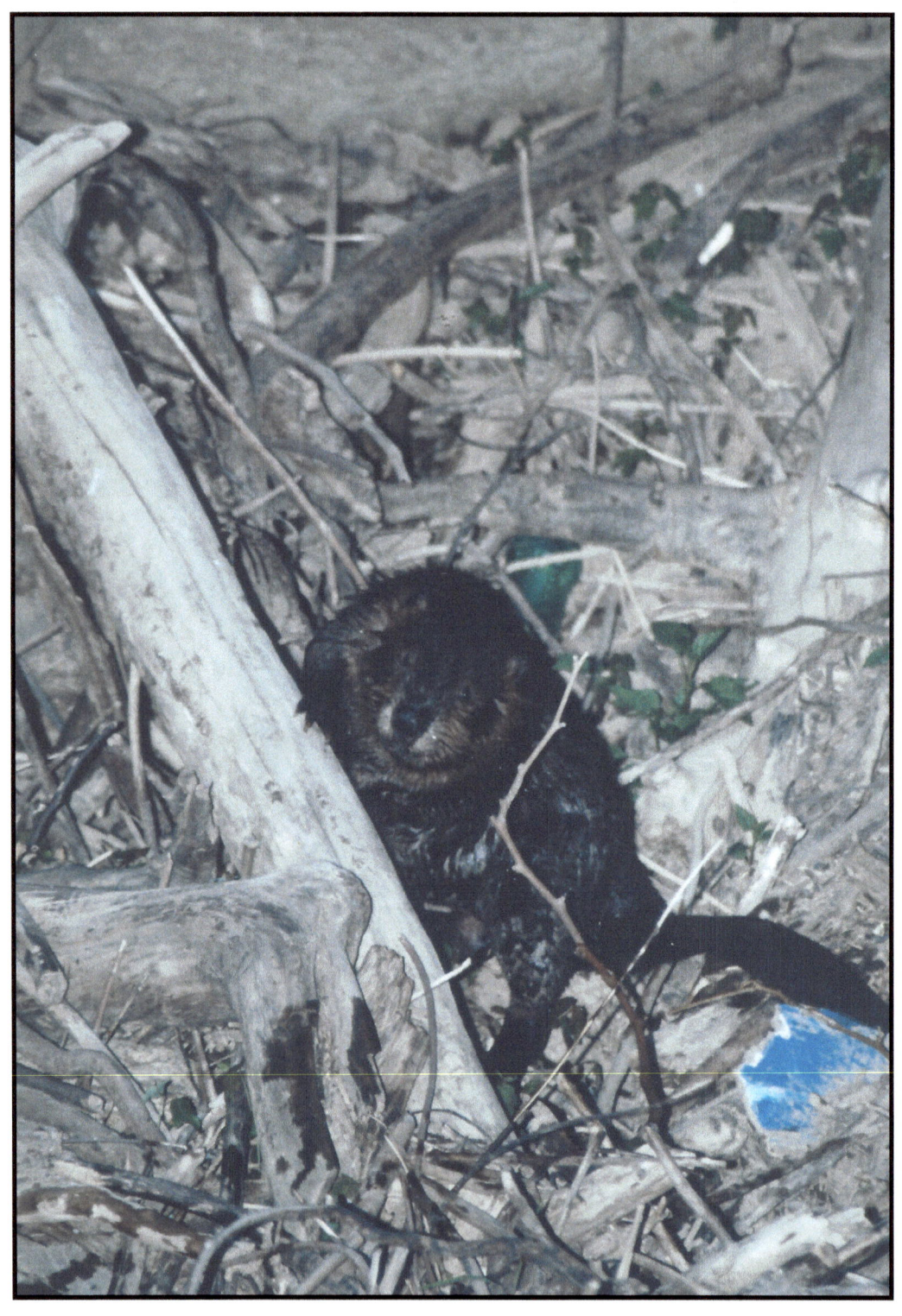

The series of pointy stumps along the roadside let us know there were beavers close by. We sat in the mid afternoon sun, looking for any signs of movement and hoping to spot one. Since neither of us knew anything about beavers, I needed to do some research.

We returned to the area less than a week later, armed with a little information. As we squished our way through the mud, the gentle waters of the creek trickled along. We found ourselves climbing over large branches and around bushes on our quest. A slight breeze drifted in the air and carried the joyful sounds of an occasional bird.

Finally, we found what we were looking for: a beaver den tucked in a secluded area only a hundred feet from the road. The beaver den resembled a large pile of sticks and branches by the water's edge. But, upon closely examining the pile, it was easy to see that each branch had been stripped of its bark. The ends were all carefully positioned and safely tucked into a definite pattern. A portion of the den was concealed below the water. There the beavers could enter and exit without being seen. It was mid-afternoon and the beavers were probably inside sleeping. We decided not to disturb them and made our way along what we thought was probably a deer trail.

Since I now knew that beavers are nocturnal, we returned to the area a few evenings later. Both Jay and I sat quietly by the creek while watching for any signs of movement.

Suddenly, there were bubbles floating to the surface, and a dark shadow beneath the water. I readied my camera and followed the shadow with the lens for quite some time. It seemed like the beaver was never going to come up for air. Then, a small black nose broke the surface of the water for only an instant, before returning to its depths. We had another fifteen minutes to wait before he had to surface again. Hopefully, next time he would be a little more daring and poke his entire head out of the water.

Jay was tired of watching the bubbles, and decided to explore the area a little more.

My eyes scanned the water surface for what seemed like an eternity. Then, finally there he was, floating along quietly just five feet from me. I zoomed in on him; my heart leapt as he changed his direction and headed right toward me. For a moment, I observed him. Only his dark brown head protruded out of the water. His long flat tail swayed from side to side to propel him along the surface.

I raised the camera to my face again, and, when I looked through the lens I realized the lighting was really bad. The sun was steadily setting, and we were nestled under a group of trees. Just as I was changing the shutter speed on the camera, the beaver submerged.

I wasn't going to get any photos of him today. We weren't far from home, and I could easily return on another day.

"Thanks anyway," I said, before going off to find Jay for our hike home.

A week later, over dinner Jay and I chatted about visiting the beavers again. He really wasn't looking forward to sitting there quietly waiting. So we decided Jay would drop me off and come back for me at a set time. We knew that being out in the woods alone wasn't a great idea, but I would be less than a mile from home, in an area I had been to several times now.

Minutes later, Jay and I said our goodbyes by the roadside, and I trekked into the woods.

Carefully, I picked my vantage point. A small hill alongside the water was the perfect spot. It would help conceal my presence from the beaver. I could easily set up my tripod to the side of it in the thick vegetation. While I was getting myself settled into a comfortable position, a stream of bubbles floated toward the surface of the water. Carefully, I peered through the lens, just in time to see a snapper turtle poke his head up. He quietly made his way to the opposite bank and I returned to scanning the small creek for any signs of the beaver.

My attention was diverted when I heard the branches of a small bush rustling nearby. Looking over, I didn't see anything, and thought it must have been a bird. Once again a series of bubbles surfaced. Below them, I could see the beaver's shadow. He was awake and hopefully going to come see me again.

As I focused in on him I suddenly became aware of the fact that I wasn't alone. To my left, I heard leaves crumpling and spotted movement in the tall grass. I wasn't sure if I should panic or if I should reposition the camera.

Before I had a chance to decide, a head popped out of the grass. There I sat, on the ground with the tripod between my legs.

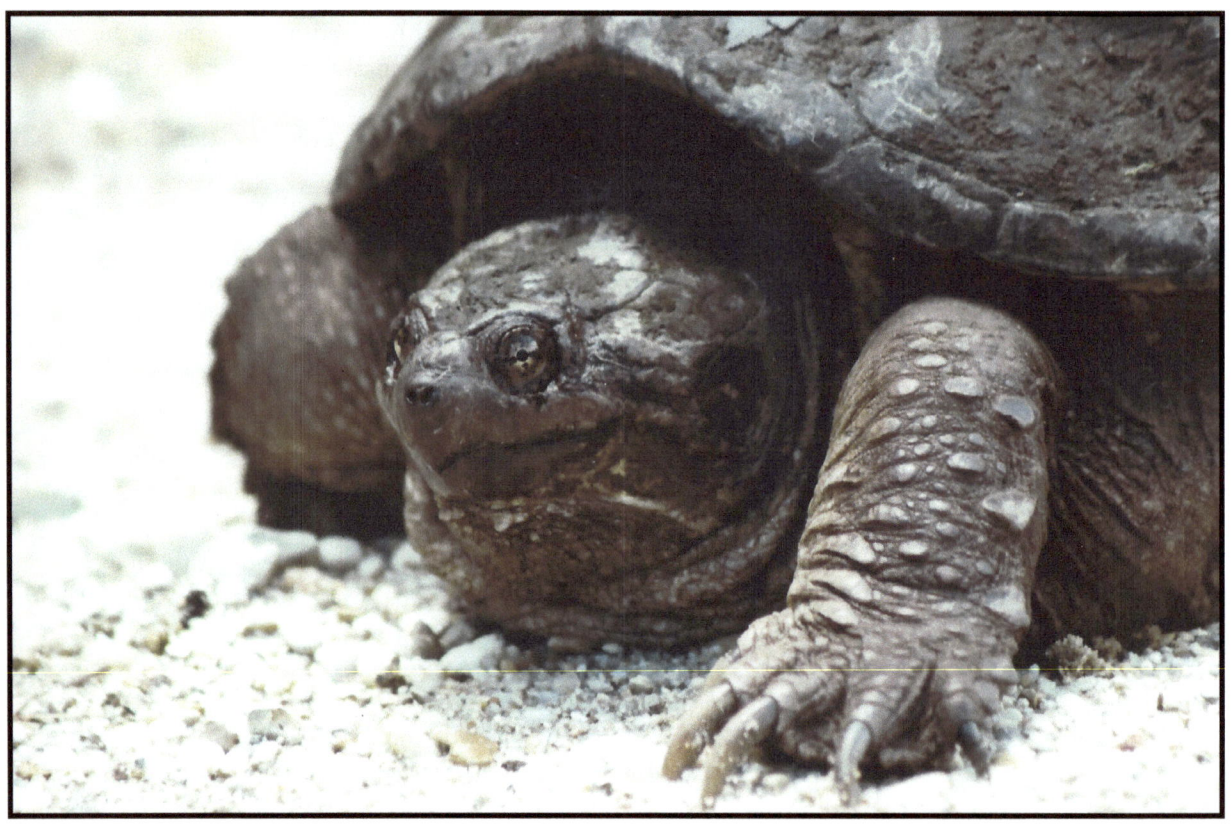

The chestnut brown, furry creature was running straight at me. His mouth was slightly opened as he approached. I could see its sharp white teeth and pink tongue. I froze as his stout legs carried him quickly toward me. The hair on the back of my neck stood straight up. He was small and cute, but I was in his territory and he could probably seriously injure me if he felt threatened. In a matter of seconds, he was just a few inches from me.

My mother's words echoed in my head. "You could be attacked by a wild animal."

Suddenly he stopped, stared right at me, turned, and plunged into the water. The entire encounter probably took only a minute or two.

Shaken, but okay, I turned my attention back to looking for the beaver. He was nowhere in sight, and it was time for me to head back to the road. Still a little shaky, I squished through the mud, and followed the tiny trail that led out of the area.

When I emerged from the trees, I spotted Jay's truck.

I climbed into the truck as a stream of cars drove by. It was amazing to me that from here, there was no sign of all the activity that was going on just a short distance away. On the short ride home, I told Jay of my encounter.

"So what was it? Did you get a picture?"

"You could ask if I was okay. I'm not sure what it was, but I plan to find out, and no, I didn't have time to get a picture."

After a quick shower, I cleaned up the kitchen and I parked myself in the living room with a stack of books. I wanted to know what kind of animal I had encountered. After paging through one book after another,

I finally identified my visitor: a mink.

I was in no real danger; he was more than likely looking for a snake or a frog to munch on. Hopefully, at our next encounter I would be able to capture him on film.

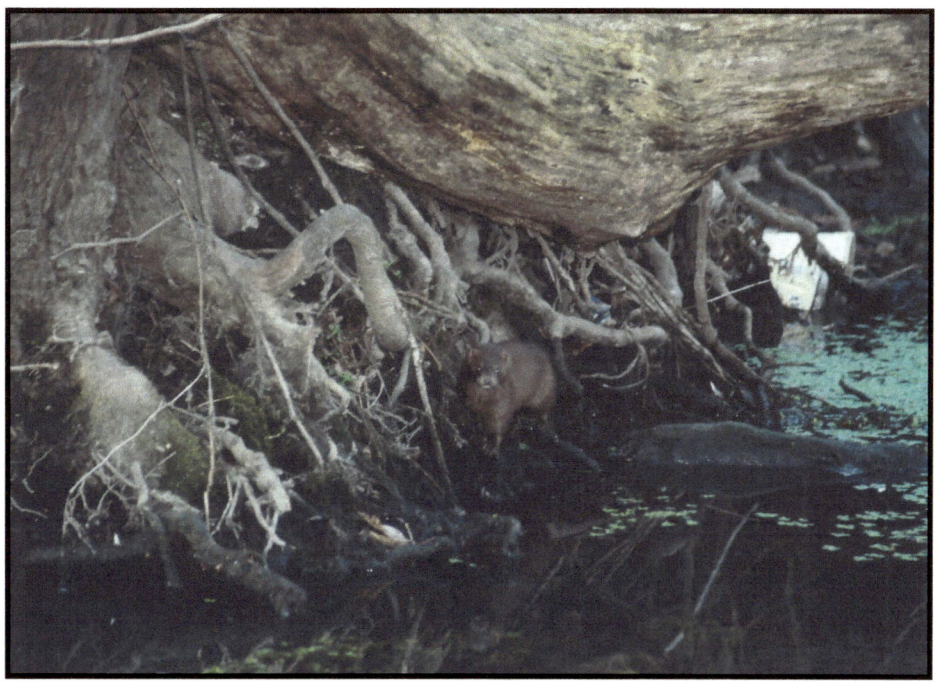

KNOT CRABBY

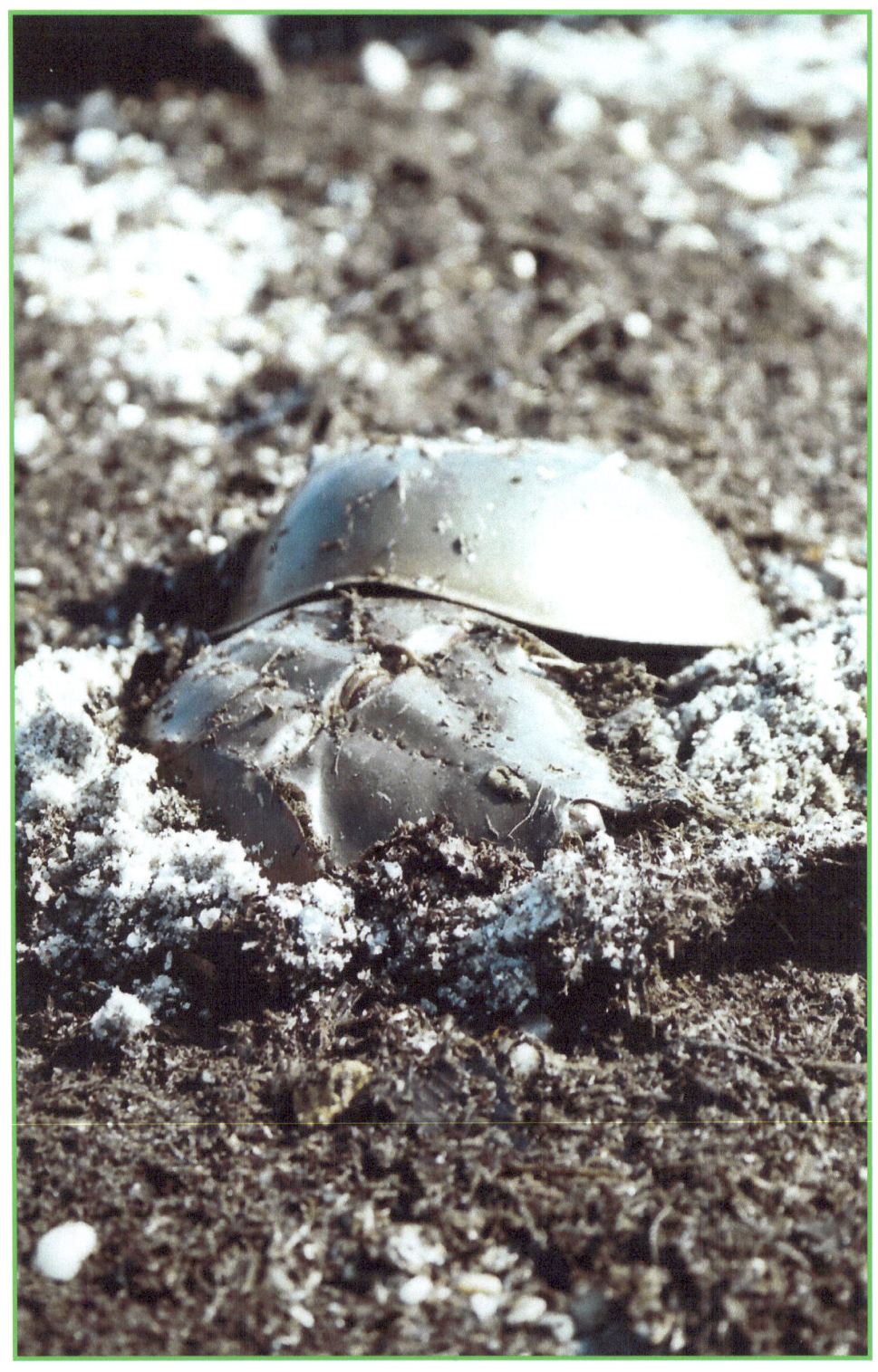

By the light of May's new moon, the invasion began. They came to leave hope for the future and a hint into the past. Making their way out of the surf and onto the sandy beaches, hundreds of Horseshoe Crabs came to lay their eggs.

My plan was to get to the beaches before all of them had returned to the surf. I wanted to capture their helmet like shells and their mass numbers on film. I wasn't the only company the crabs would have. Hundreds and hundreds of shore birds would also be at the beaches. Their plan was to dine on the Horseshoe Crab eggs.

At four in the morning, Jay and I started the long journey to the shores of the Delaware Bay. We had maps, notes, and a semi-plan. If our timing was good, we would not only see Horseshoe Crabs, but also a wide variety of birds, including Red Knots. The Red Knots stop to gorge on the Horseshoe Crab eggs before continuing on their long journey from one end of the earth to the other.

We arrived at our first destination, a wildlife refuge, at dawn. We traveled along the dirt roads that offered an auto tour of the area. The varied landscape proved to be appealing to a number of different critters. As we drove along looking for cooperative critters to photograph, a mud turtle made its way onto the road.

The little guy was about the size of my fist, and a bit apprehensive. When I first approached him, he quickly retreated into his shell. Lying on the ground, I softly asked him to come out and have his picture taken. After a bit of hesitation, he began to poke his head out. I zoomed in his tan face, which was dotted with hundreds of dark splotches. Placing my chin on the ground, I refocused and snapped off another shot that included his dark shell.

On the opposite side of the road was a blue grosbeck. His white beak seemed out of place next to the black markings that adorned his face. The deep blue feathers that covered his body made him easy to see, even on a cloudy day like today. He was happy to perch and wait for me to get a few pictures. He even let me walk a little closer, then closer still, before flying off.

There were a variety of song birds and even a shy raccoon at the refuge, but no access to the beaches. So we moved on to another location.

We found them on a quiet beach outside of town. Although we had missed the massive influx of Horseshoe Crabs, there were still plenty of them to photograph. Walking along the sandy shore, I was saddened to find most of the crabs that remained were upside down. Sharp, dagger-like tails protruded into the air, dotting the shore line. Often, Horseshoe Crabs get flipped over by a wave and they are unable to get themselves upright on land. Their only chance for survival was to hope the next high tide would toss them back on their feet. Since high tide was more than four hours away, I gave them a hand.

When approaching the first upside down Horseshoe Crab, I noticed its multiple dark legs, which reminded me of a spider. The poor thing wasn't moving much, probably tired from hours of attempting to flip itself over. I simply grabbed hold of the underside of a shell and turned it over. Almost immediately, the crab began walking toward the water.

"Wait a minute, I want to get your picture!" I shouted.

Knot Crabby

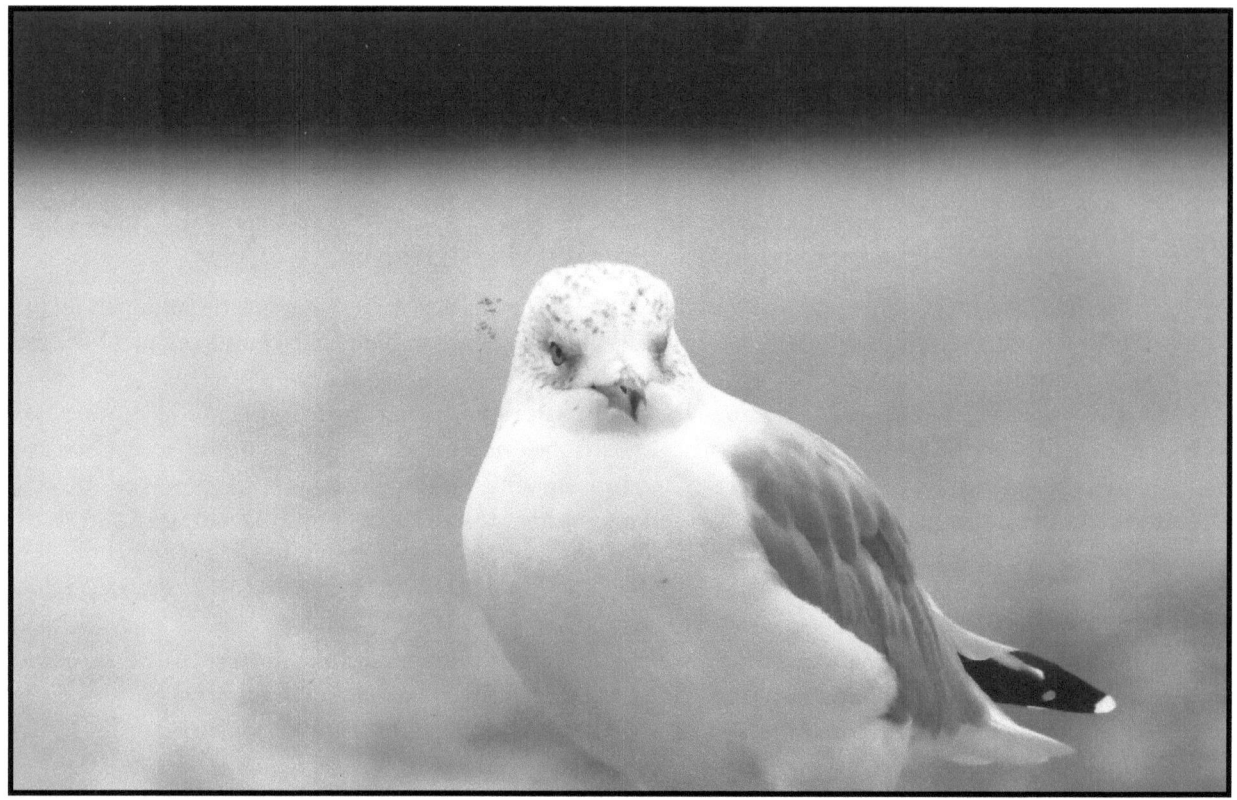

Undeterred, the Horseshoe Crab continued on its journey, and I moved on to the next one. Gently, I turned over crab after crab, even those that appeared to be dead. One by one, they marched toward the surf.

Finally, I took a moment to get a few pictures.

My first subject was covered with a mix of sand, and pebbles. I focused in on one dark marble-like eye and recorded the experience as it crawled past me. I couldn't believe how big this crab's shell was. This was on old timer, who would hopefully return again next year. The mix of tan and olive green coloring on its armor-like shell filled the lens as I depressed the shutter button. It is amazing to me that such an unattractive creature could be so important. The survival of the endangered Red Knots and other shore birds depended on the eggs of the Horseshoe Crabs.

The crab's blue blood was collected and used for medical purposes. These guys were an important link in the chain of life.

Darting across the landscape were hundreds of sandpipers, plovers, and similar shore birds. They pocked their beaks into the wet sands of the low tide, searching for a morsel or two. It was time to focus on that flock and hope to see a Red Knot or two.

As I turned to observe the army of Horseshoe Crabs making their way across the sand, I felt a sense of accomplishment. I quickly framed in the scene before turning my attention to the birds.

I zoomed out a bit to get a shot of the flock that had assembled off to our right. They seemed to shift in unison from one section of the sand to another. Slowly, I moved toward them and took another shot.

Refocusing, I concentrated on a single bird at the edge of the flock. Its reddish brown back feathers were dotted with black accents. Its tiny, straw-like legs emerged from the murky sand while its long beak poked beneath the surface in search of a snack. I stepped closer to get a better view, prompting the entire flock to scurry to another area. Each time I attempted to move closer, they would drift further away. I knelt, in an attempt to get closer to the birds without startling them, and depressed the shutter button.

Raindrops began to tap me on the shoulder as I evaluated the situation. The birds weren't happy I was there, and the weather was deteriorating. Maybe it was time to head for home.

Jay began shouting at me, but it was difficult to hear him above the roar of the waves. Then he pointed to a lone crab flailing in the surf in an attempt to flip over.

His squirming legs seemed to be coaxing me to lend him a hand. Making my way closer, I noticed the spongy texture of the sand beneath my feet, but I kept going. Then suddenly my entire foot was sucked into the muddy sand. While attempting to pull myself free, I managed to get my foot loose, but my shoe remained buried. Standing on one leg, I bent over to retrieve my shoe. Of course, I lost my balance quickly. I put my hand out to try to break my fall. I didn't fall over, but now my hand had disappeared into the mud. It took a few minutes but I managed to free myself.

With my shoe in one hand and my camera in the other, I made my way, inch-by-inch, to the distraught Horseshoe Crab.

"Looks like you could use a little help," I said as I flipped him over.

He immediately crawled toward the water. Further down the beach, the surface was a bit firmer and I was able to walk without sinking. I took a minute to splash in the surf and clean off my hands, feet, and shoes, before returning with Jay to the truck.

It was now raining steadily, and we weren't going to be able to get any closer to the birds without disturbing them, so we headed for home.

I wasn't able to get any really good shots of Red Knots, but we enjoyed our time with the Horseshoe Crabs and would return again next year.

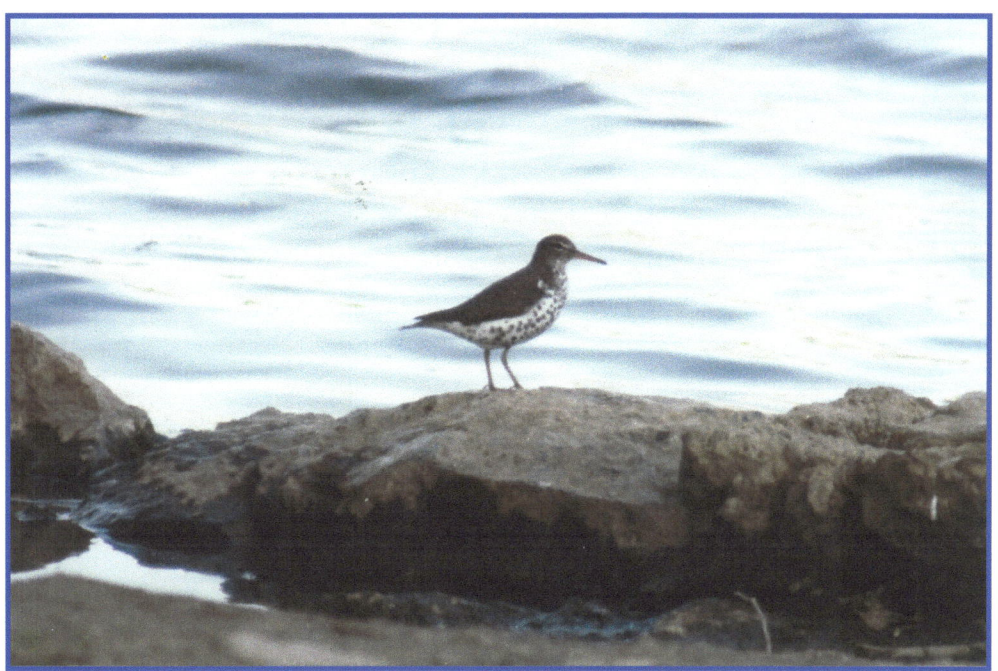

A WILD RIDE

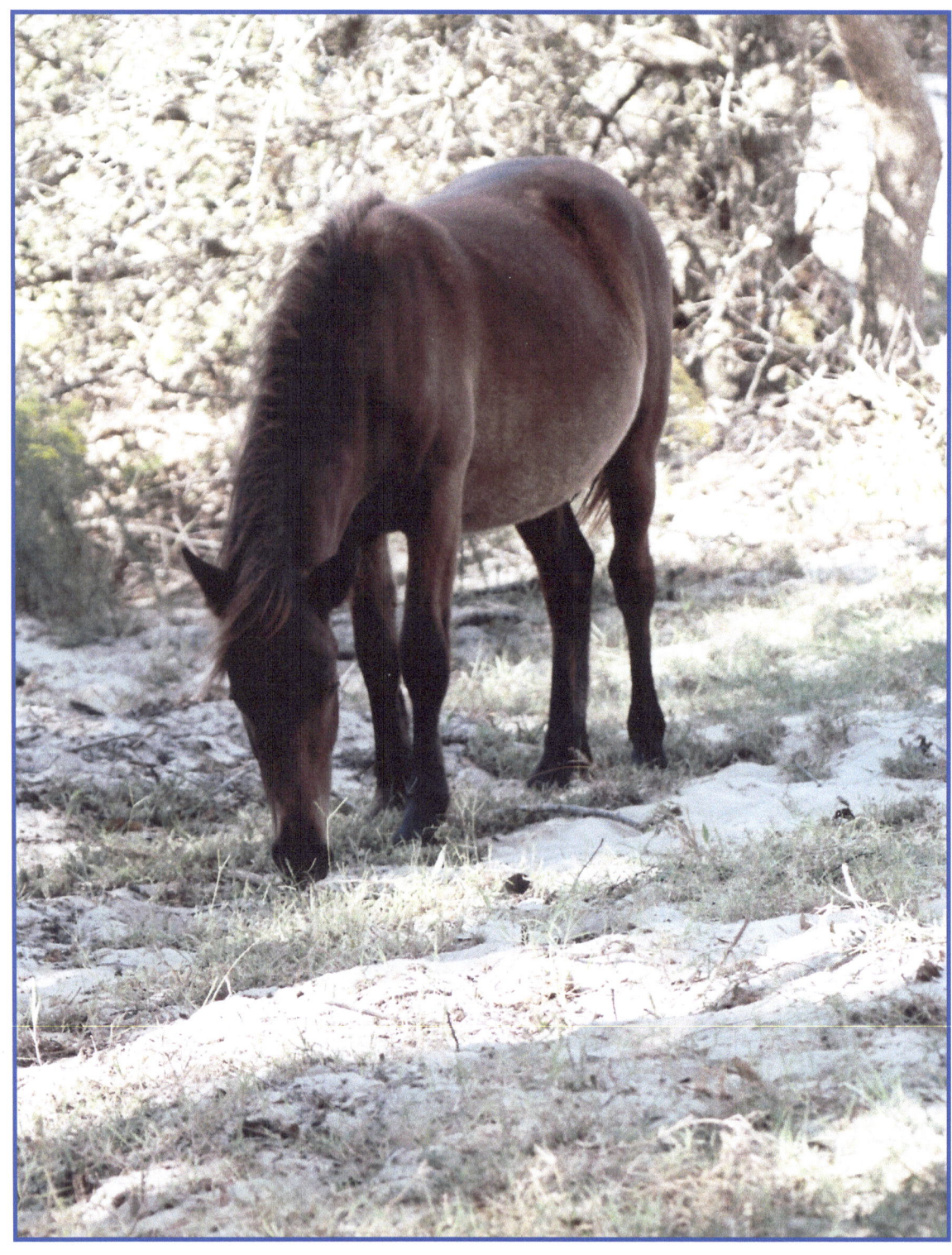

The locations I choose for photographing wildlife are usually on public lands or, occasionally, on private property, when I can get permission. Generally, I don't include tourist attractions or guided tours. However, when exploring an area that I am unfamiliar with, I may have to resort to taking advantage of these types of venues. Of course, I do my own research, and combine that with the information provided through the tour to help me find the critters I am hoping to photograph.

Jay and I had learned about a small herd of wild mustangs that, with a little effort, we could find and photograph. First, we needed a four-wheel drive vehicle. The area the mustangs called home required a drive along the beach. I went on the Internet and explored our options. Most places in that area that would rent us what we needed offered weekly rates. We wouldn't be staying for a week, so I was down to only a few choices. Being unfamiliar with any of the businesses, I just picked one.

We sat quietly in a brief class with five or six other people, and were instructed on how to properly maneuver a vehicle in the sand. Our instructor offered a few hints on where the horses might be found, and cautioned us about trespassing on private property. Then we were given a map and the keys to our chariot for the day. It was an older model Jeep, with the top and doors removed.

Our map provided us with good directions through town, and took us right to the beach access location for vehicles. From there, we were on our own.

There were deep ruts in the sand left by other outdoor enthusiasts. This, in addition recent storms in the area, made the sand wet and tricky to navigate. This was where our adventure truly began.

It wasn't long before I was exiting the jeep to photograph one of the many shore birds we spotted. The aroma of the sea air engulfed me. While I focused, clicked, and changed angles, Jay noticed a problem with the Jeep. The rough ride we had experienced on our way here wasn't due to the reduced air pressure in the tires as we had thought. As the vehicle idled, it was vibrating more than expected. Once I returned to the Jeep, we concluded that it was an old vehicle and wasn't going to run smoothly all the time, so we continued on our quest.

We spotted our first sign that mustangs had been in the area: an ample pile of horse scat. We knew we were on the right track.

As we maneuvered along the sandy surface, a brisk breeze floated off the ocean. The sounds of the surf, combined with being tussled from side to side, made conversation difficult.

Just as we spotted our first hoof print, the Jeep jumped out of four wheel drive. Fortunately, Jay had a bit of knowledge about off road vehicles. After several tense moments, Jay was able to get the four-wheel drive working again, but he had to hold the leaver in place while driving.

Following the prints, we were led off the beach and onto a path that led through a wooded area. This was easier terrain to navigate, and we began to relax a bit. As we proceeded down the rugged path, I got out from time-to-time to locate the next hoof print. The mustangs were roaming off to the sides, and then returning to the path. While I was scanning the surface for the next telltale sign, Jay noticed movement beyond the trees.

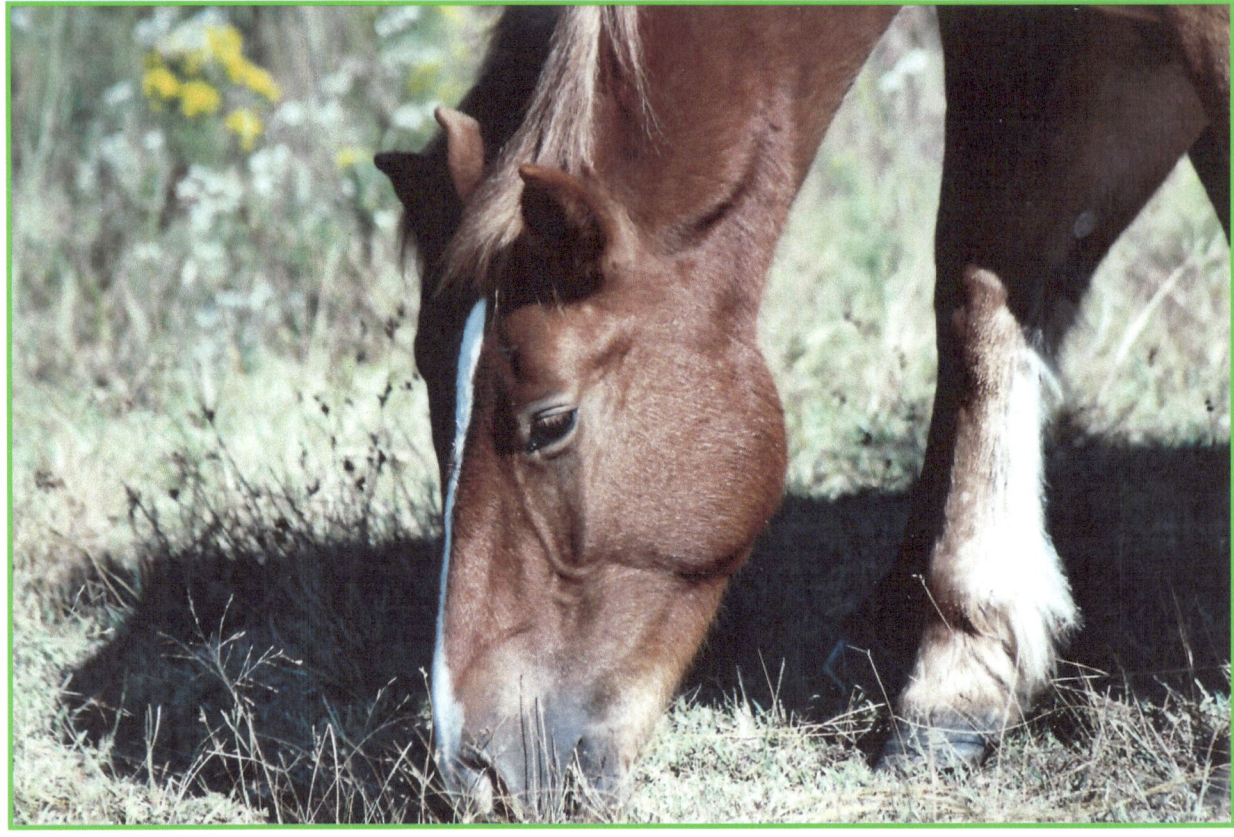

We couldn't quite make out what it was. It appeared the path we were following wound its way to the area, so we slowly proceeded in that direction.

Then, like magic, there they were. Two chestnut brown mustangs were carelessly munching on Mother Nature's offerings.

Careful not to disturb them, I timidly placed one foot in front of the other. Picking a location behind a tree, I clicked off a few frames of film. One of them swished its tail from side to side. I was sure this would appear as a blur in the photograph, so I adjusted the shutter speed. Inching closer, I depressed the shutter button again.

While my spirits were being lifted by this tranquil scene, Jay's anxiety was steadily building. The temperature gauge in the jeep was creeping higher; this wasn't good. We were miles from civilization, and it would be a long walk back.

Leaving the horses grazing in the midday sun, I returned to the Jeep. Jay and I discussed our options, and thought we should start making our way back to town while we could. I was disappointed, but hoped we would encounter a few more Mustangs on our way.

With a bit of careful driving, Jay was able to get the old Jeep turned around, and I took one more shot before the mustangs were out of sight.

Jay noticed that we were once again following hoof prints, only these horses were in front of us somewhere. I might get a chance to get a few more shots after all. Soon, five new subjects, including a yearling, emerged. Like the others, these horses seemed undisturbed by my presence.

Although they looked docile enough, I had to remind myself these were wild animals. Not only were there laws against getting too close to them, but they could also suddenly decide I was a threat.

Kneeling down, I focused in on the herd. The thick muscular leg of one horse stomped the ground in an attempt to chase away an annoying fly. A few members of the group grazed in the sun, while others opted for a shadier location. I wanted to get all of them on film. As I finished off a roll of film, the youngest of the group began to approach me.

This could be a great opportunity or an invitation to disaster. I was about to see just how tolerant the mother horse was. Mom took a step in my direction, just to let me know she was there. I quickly reloaded while I weighed my options. I depressed the shutter button a few times before retreating back to the Jeep.

As I suspected, this would be our last encounter before Jay coaxed the old Jeep back toward civilization. We welcomed each passing mile as the vehicle sputtered and coughed. Finally, we were back on the paved surface. Just a few miles through town and we would be there. When we arrived back at the rental location we were happy.

The previously friendly, helpful associate didn't seem too concerned. He was filled with excuses about it being off season for tourist, and these things happen. The end result was they had my money and I only had two rolls of images instead of my anticipated seven or eight rolls.

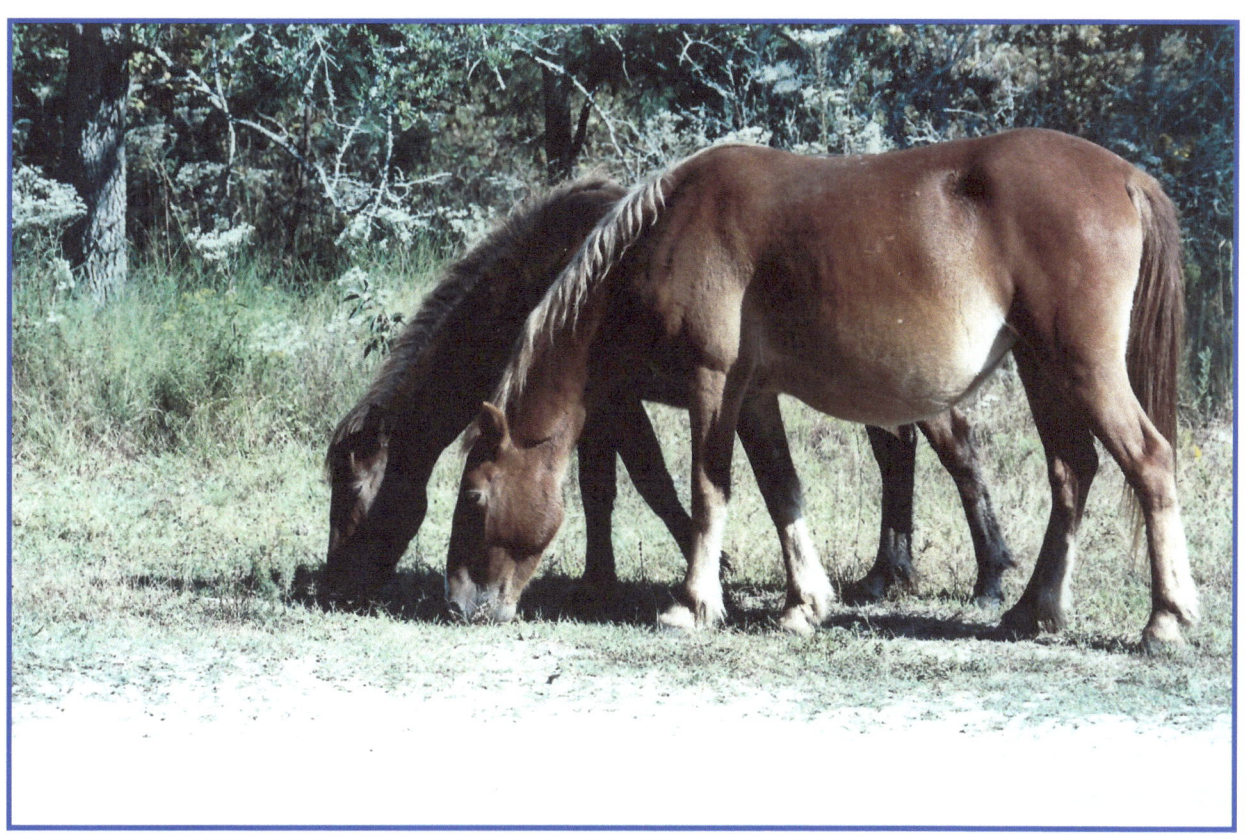

FOLLOWING FEATHERS

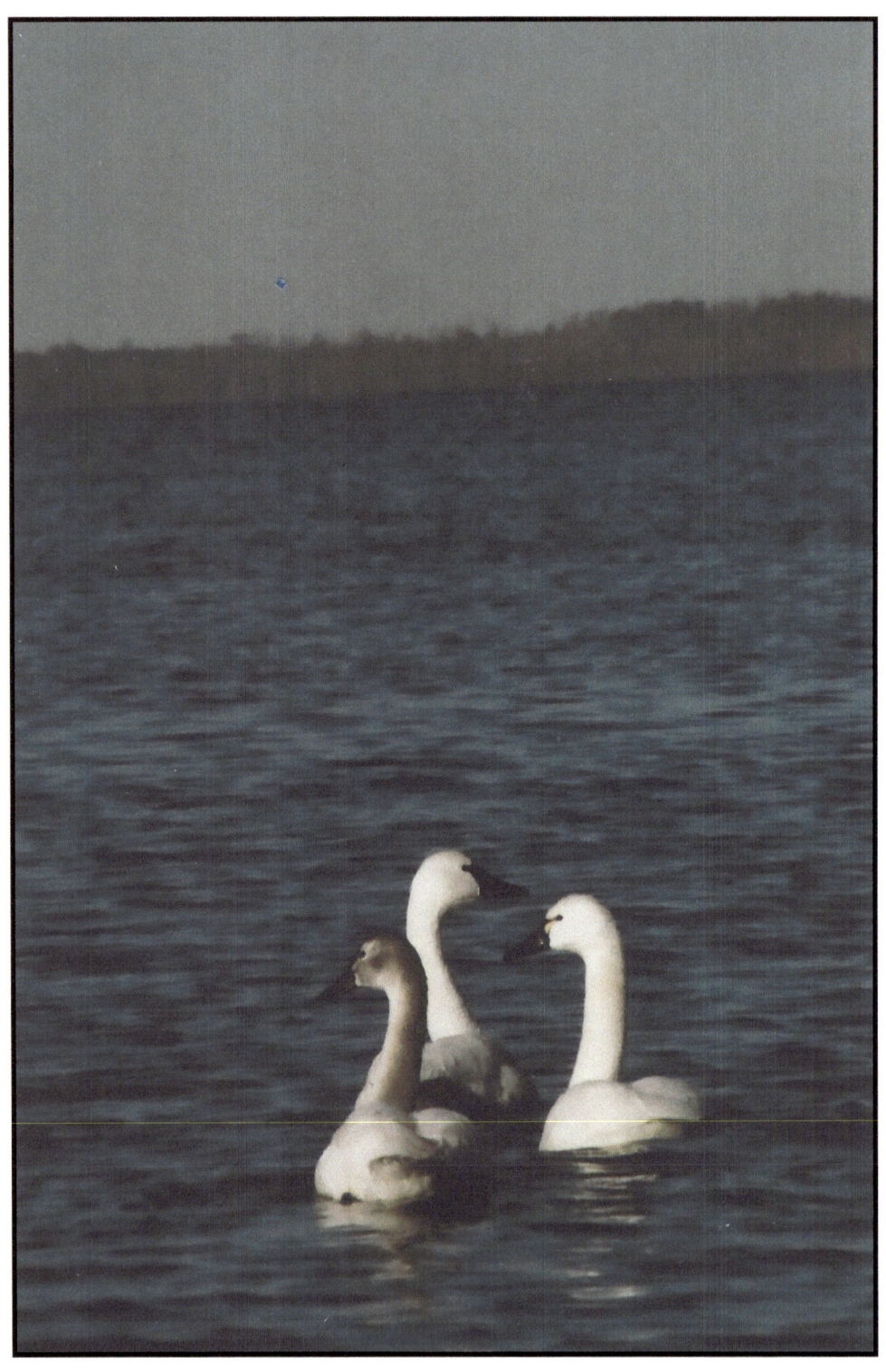

Traveling along the snow covered streets in the predawn hours, I understand why so many birds opt for warmer climates. This trip would take us in search of migrating birds. Animals that move from place to place can be challenging to find and photograph. I have to consider current and past weather conditions, as well as annual routes. Also, our feathered friends don't utilize colorful wall calendars; they instead have an internal calendar all their own.

Therefore, all the useful data I collect and store and all the experts that I consult with only offer a guestimate of when and where the migrating birds will appear. Now how long they will stay in a given location is determined by only a few important factors: food, water, and safety being the most important to them.

Our current destination is an area known to be a winter gathering place for Bald Eagles. Everyone has a wild animal they relate to, and for me it is wolves: they are illusive, strong, truly untamed creatures; for Jay, it's Bald Eagles.

It was early February, during one of the coldest winters I could remember in quite some time. Between us and the Bald Eagles were several large cities, a number of small towns, lots of traffic, and hours and hours of driving, but we were on our way.

Once on the interstate, we joined the mass of early morning commuters. Driving along, we passed an array of chain stores, shopping malls, and office buildings.   A classic rock station serenaded us during the drive. As the miles and the hours slowly passed, we discussed our strategy for the morning. We would don layers of warm clothing and set out to explore the lake where the Bald Eagles were known to congregate. I would look for a location that allowed me to photograph our white headed friends without disturbing their morning routine. Generally, a large tree or bush did the trick. Jay would scan the horizon, while I examined the tree lined shores. Our true hope was that the eagles would be in large numbers and easily spotted.

While we searched for a good location to stop for lunch, we found something quite unexpected. Among the usual fast food restaurants, car dealerships, and strip malls was a castle. I never thought of Kentucky as an area where I would see such a medieval looking structure. However, proudly perched on the top of a knoll was real honest-to-goodness castle. Protruding above the massive stone walls were a number of towers. Some had cone-like pointed roofs, while others appeared to be like rooftop terraces. The huge wooden gates that guarded the entrance appeared old and weather by time.

This was worth a closer look, and maybe a quick photograph or two before continuing on our way. As I paused to get a few pictures, I was reminded of the giant roller skate I had photographed last year. Then, I thought about the building shaped like an elephant that captured our attention in another state. Finding unusual sights along our route always helped to break up the trip

Shortly after sunset, we neared our destination.

The town was eerily dark, and seemed uninviting. No pedestrians wandered from shop to shop. No cars waited at the only stop sign in town. Then like a bright beacon in the night, we spotted the motel sign. We soon learned an ice storm had ravaged the area, and our accommodations were one of the few locations where power had been restored. That meant the offerings at local eateries and grocery stores would be very limited, so we were glad we added a cooler full of food to the back of the truck.

Our room was clean and warm, and we settled in to pour over maps of the area and revise our plans for in the morning. Before turning in for the night, I checked the weather forecast. Morning would bring sunshine and milder temperatures, according to the weatherman with the bad toupee and bow tie. I was hoping that he was right.

Morning brought bitter cold temperatures and biting winds. I retrieved my insulated underwear from the duffel bag. I added a hooded sweatshirt over my top and zipped up my heavy jeans. When the windows began to rattle, I opted for two pairs of socks under my insulated boots. As the wind howled outside our door, I pulled my hood up over my hat, added a second pair of gloves, took a deep breath, and ventured out.

Jay, on the other hand, filled his thermos with coffee, put on a jacket, and grabbed a pair of gloves before following me.

Bracing ourselves against the wind, we proceeded slowly toward the nearby lake.

While the sun rose, a hungry squirrel rustled around in the leaf litter looking for a morsel or two. Finally, he scampered out from beneath the trees and into the open. There he discovered a tiny treat to satisfy his appetite.

For what seemed like hours, we watched and waited for the Bald Eagles to take to the skies. We began to suspect reports of the numerous Bald Eagle sightings here were greatly exaggerated. It was possible that the recent onset of cold weather may have coaxed them to stay further south. Either way, our prime location wasn't very prime. Our big find for the morning was that hungry squirrel, so we decided to go exploring.

A steady stream of air bellowed from the heat vents and slowly warmed us as we removed our boots and wiggled our toes. While we toured a few back country roads, I retrieved the bag of snacks that was stashed behind the seat. Munching on donuts, we scanned the fields and wooded areas searching for local critters.

When we rounded a bend, a flock of black vultures came into view. They had perched themselves in an old dead tree. A mass of coal colored feathers fluttered in the wind as I stepped out of the truck. The startled birds took to the sky, resembling a huge dark cloud as they floated off.

I was delighted to find a few brave souls had remained clamped to their perches. While I approached, they nervously shifted their weight from side to side. Pausing for a moment, I let them get used to my presence before I clicked the shutter button. Using a tree to block their view of me, I inched closer before depressing the shutter button again. Stepping forward, I focused in on their razor like talons. This was just a little too close for comfort, and the large raptures took to the air.

As we proceeded, it seemed that with the exception of some power company workers, we were the only ones braving the cold on this sunny winter day. There were no signs of any geese, deer, or even small birds along our route.

Then we discovered an access road that led us onto the levy system along the Mississippi river. Driving along the dirt path that topped off the levy, we looked down at farm fields on one side and tree tops on the other. Even with this elevated vantage point, we still hadn't seen any Bald Eagles. Then, just beyond a stand of trees, Jay spied a Bald Eagle in her nest. We were only able to see her stark white head protruding above the massive structure. A strong wind encompassed the area, causing the tree branches to dance. This made it difficult to get a decent view of her, and nearly impossible to take her picture. Walking to the edge of the trees, I clicked off a few shots before we went on our way.

Later in the day, we came across a few fellow bird watchers. During our conversion, we learned they came each year from the other side of the state to see the eagles. They offered us little bits of insight that hopefully would make our trip more successful. Half an hour later, we were headed to a location our new friends had visited in past years.

Pulling off the side of the road, we glanced down a path that led beyond the trees. Before I even zipped my jacket, Jay was out of the truck. While I was putting on my gloves, he made his way down the path.

Once outside, I could hear him screaming, "There's one. Look there's another one. "

When I cleared the last row of trees, I saw him standing in the middle of the field pointing toward the sky.

Shivering in the cold, I clicked off frame after frame while Jay pointed and counted. I captured a juvenile Bald Eagle in one frame and an adult a moment later. While the camera rewound another roll of film, I realized Jay hadn't even put his jacket on.

I walked up on an eagle perched in a tree, but that bird didn't want its picture taken. Then, about halfway through the next roll of film, I realized Jay had slippers on. There he stood, in the freezing cold, as excited as a five year old that had seen his first shooting star.

Stark white heads approached the field from several directions.

Zoom, focus, click. Zoom, focus, click. I repeated this process numerous times. When Jay counted, he spotted thirteen different Bald Eagles in the sky above him at one time. This was why we came. Eventually the birds moved on to another location and we returned to the truck.

Another search for migrating birds took us south east into North Carolina. We were hoping to find Tundra Swans and snow geese. Once again, we had a short window of opportunity to see the birds. They would fly in for a few weeks and fuel up before heading on their way.

You may be thinking, "Swans, geese, oh yeah I see them at the park and they walk right up to me. How hard can it be to photograph a bunch of them?"

The swans I was going to see were not only wild birds, but they migrated as well. This means they don't equate people with food like the swans at the park. Instead, to them people mean danger. They generally stay in outlying areas and have very little contact with people. This makes them leery and not at all cooperative when it comes to being photographed.

We began our first morning out in a wildlife refuge and found a few hundred birds. Mixed in with the swans and geese were ducks and coots.

To zoom in and get some decent shots, I would need to test their tolerance a bit.

The coots paddled along the water's edge looking for food. Slowly, I crept toward the water and knelt down. Focusing in on the bird's bright red eyes, I clicked the shutter button.

My new found friend glanced in my direction long enough for me to zoom in on its white beak and click off another frame. Drifting slowly away, the coot turned and offered me a butt shot.

It was time to get a little closer to a nearby group of swans. They decided that wasn't such a good idea and quickly paddled away.

After several attempts, I took a break from pursuing the swans. They were very leery of me and wanted no part of having their picture taken.

I had managed to get what I considered scenic shots that included the swans, but not the close-up shots I was after.

Just before sunset, I found a new vantage point. Sitting behind a row of trees along the water's edge, I zoomed in on a small group of swans. I clicked off frame after frame while trying not to be discovered by these delicate creatures.

Following Feathers

The adults' bodies were covered with delicate white feathers that fluttered in the breeze. Their large black feet slowly paddled below the surface of the water. The juveniles' feathers were a mix of white and light tan, with charcoal coloring on their necks and head. They were a bit more relaxed than the adults and uttered bugling sounds to one another. The flapping of their black beaks made them a challenge to capture on film.

As the day progressed, we visited several other locations. We searched swamps, ponds, and lakes throughout the region. The snow geese turned out to be much easier subjects. They seemed curious, but a bit leery as well; however the marshy areas they preferred were a bit trickier to maneuver around in.

By the time I returned to the truck, I had several good images and mud caked up around my ankles.

Darkness slowly encompassed the area and Jay and I headed back to town. After a bit to eat and a hot shower, we turned in early. We would head back to the first lake we had visited in the morning, and hope that maybe the swans would be a bit more cooperative.

In the morning, we returned to the lake and I parked myself on the grass. Jay sat in the truck sipping on a steaming hot cup of coffee and looking over maps of the area. To our surprise, most of the swans had left the area before we had arrived. Today, there were only a few white objects visible in the center of the large lake.

Several mallard ducks remained close to shore, so I focused in on them. Sunlight reflected on the emerald green coloring on a male mallard's head. I could see hints of blue and black shading in the feathers.

Just as I was about to press the shutter button, he let out an alarm call. Suddenly, water was splashing everywhere. Loud honks filled the air and the entire flock took flight. I quickly changed the camera settings and followed them with the lens. All the splashing and honking got Jay's attention, and he joined me at the water edge as the birds faded from view.

Glancing back at the lake, I saw calm water and a few reeds swaying in the wind, but not a single swan, goose, duck, or coot.

It was time to head home and be grateful for the images I did manage to capture.

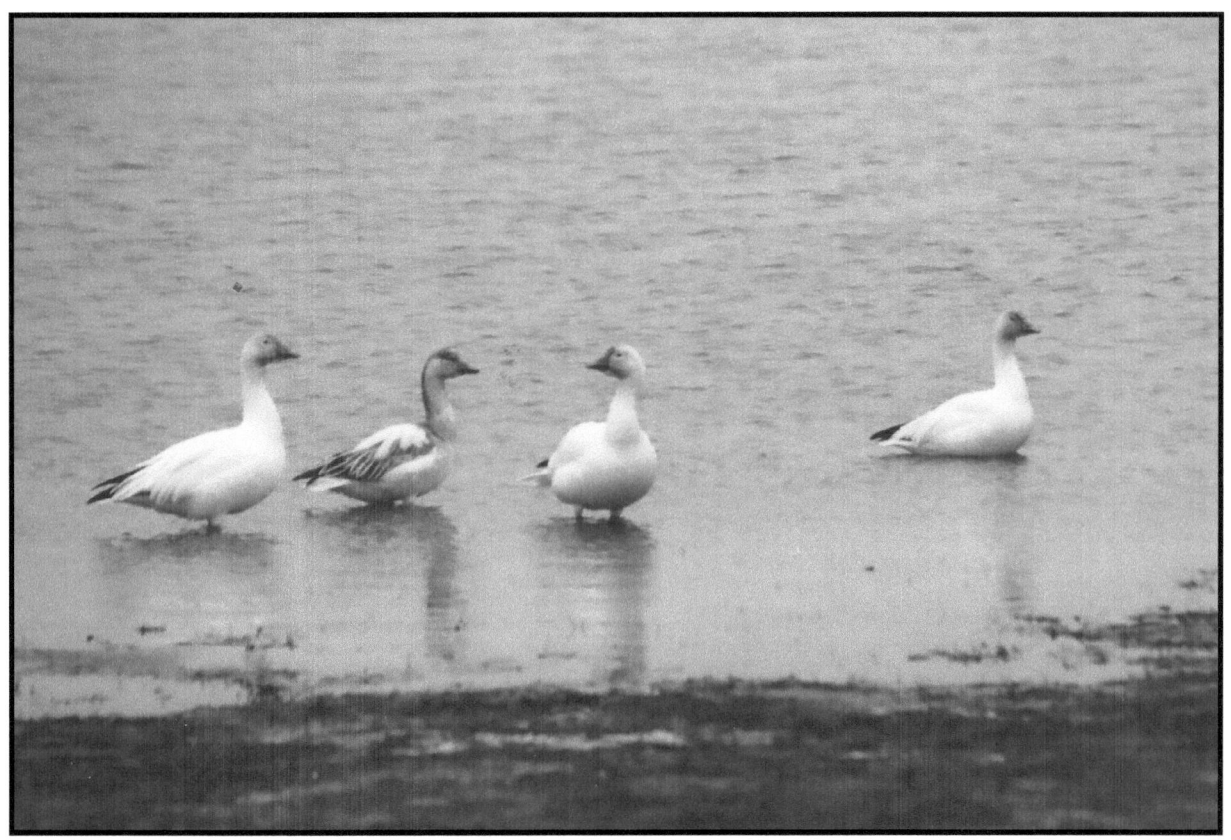

THIS PLACE IS FOR THE BIRDS

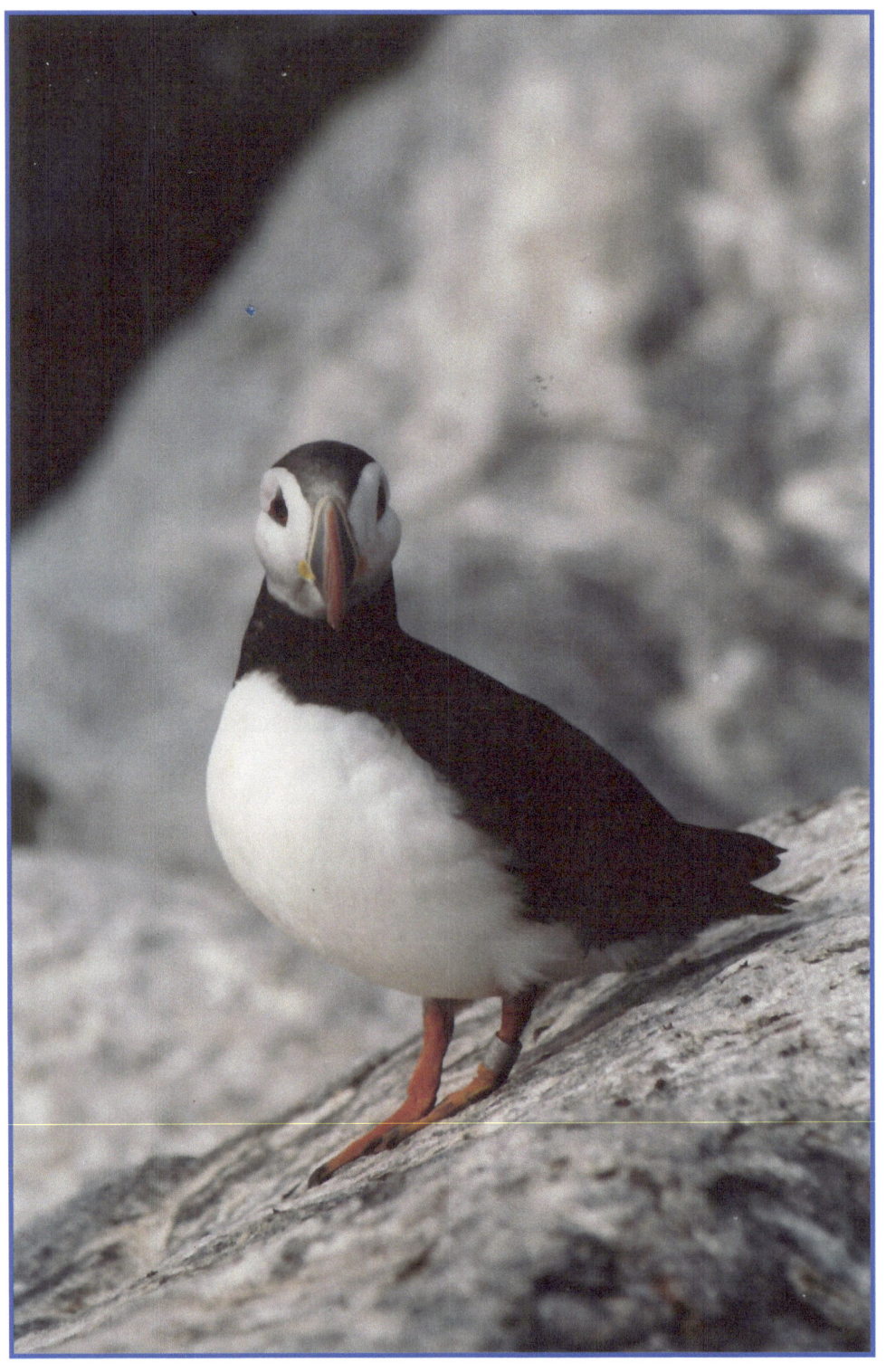

With a wave of his hand, the first mate let me know we were close to our destination. Soon, the roar of the engine stopped and the next leg of our journey would begin. Apprehensively, I looked over the side as the waves slapped at our boat. Swaying in the surf was the waiting row boat.

Jay slowly maneuvered himself into the battered-looking vessel. I handed him my camera bag, took a deep breath, and stepped down to join him. Nervously, I gripped the sides of the old wooden boat while the captain guided us to the rocky shore.

Dense fog covered the island, giving the area an eerie feel, as the sounds of its inhabitants filled the air.

After nearly a year of planning, we had arrived. We made our way over the slippery, wet rocks and onto the island. We were greeted by a conservation officer and reminded of the regulations we were required to follow while there. We were intruders and needed to watch every step we made.

We would be escorted at all times, and were not permitted to explore the island. Traveling down the narrow path, we needed to walk gingerly. There was always a possibility of finding a baby chick or egg, since these birds nested on the ground and in the rocks. We would go directly to a duck blind, and once there, we were to enter and stay inside at all times. Our visit would last no more than three hours. Touching the birds, or approaching or harassing them in any way was strictly forbidden.

There were quite a number of rules and regulations, but I didn't care. We were finally here. Not only was I back on solid ground, I was yards away from a colony of Atlantic Puffins.

Slowly and quietly, we made our way toward the duck blind.

All around us, on the ground and on the rock ledges, were dozens and dozens of puffins. Their pitch-black backs and white bellies were a strange contrast to their bright orange feet and multicolored bills. They waddled about nervously when we wandered into the group. The pungent odor of fish engulfed us as we neared our destination.

Once inside the blind, Jay and I stood quietly for a moment to let the reality of where we were sink in. We were a long way from our friends and neighbors back home in West Virginia. Then, we quietly opened one peek hole after another and peered out.

Gradually, the puffins calmed down and resumed their activities. We marveled at how close we were to the birds. Jay commented on the thick, cumbersome looking red, black, and yellow beaks of the birds while I focused in one. We spoke in whispers as more and birds emerged from the ceiling of fog and landed close by.

Some were enjoying their reward from a successful fishing trip, while others stashed their catch in the rocks. A few birds lay on the cold, hard rocks with their beaks tucked into their back feathers, quietly slumbering. I wandered how they could possible sleep with all the noise and activity around them. I spotted one bird flying in with some fish. He didn't exactly glide in for a landing, but rather stumbled to a halt. Then he shook himself off and waddled to his nest site.

This Place Is for the Birds

Click, click went the camera, as a puffin poked his head out of a cavern in the rocks. I zoomed in on a pair tugging at a small fish. There were puffins everywhere. Groups were gathered on top of the rocks, and lone individuals were scattered throughout the area.

While I clicked off picture after picture, Jay repeatedly whispered to me.

"Look at this one,"

"Did you see that one?"

"Get a picture of this."

I was reloading the camera when the door to the blind opened. It was the first mate coming to inform us we had to leave. It had only been a little more than an hour, but the seas were getting rough, and we needed to get off the island. Quickly, I gathered up my camera equipment and followed our escort through the colony.

Wandering down the narrow path, I studied each bird I passed. As they scurried about, we made our way away from the birds. I paused for a moment and turned around for one last glance.

"Thanks, guys," I whispered while the first mate nudged me toward the shoreline.

Getting off the island was a bit tougher than getting on. We made our way back toward the shore. Once on the steep wet rocks, we could see the captain wrestling with the boat in the tough surf.

The first mate hollered instructions to us as the waves crashed into the rocks. He urged us to get as close to the water as we could. Then the captain would try to land the boat. We were led further and further out onto the wet rocks. The wind whipped at our clothes while the pounding surf sprayed us. The waiting rowboat lurched from side to side as we approached. The motor on the old boat strained and whined as it came closer.

"Grab the front of the boat," the captain hollered.

The first mate leaned forward and reached for the boat. It was jumping about in the surf and he couldn't get hold of it. Then a giant wave tossed the boat out of his reach. While the first mate regained his footing, the captain fought the current and maneuvered the boat back toward the rocks. The first mate managed to grab the tip of the boat and pull it toward us.

"Hurry up, get to the boat," he screamed at us.

Jay paused for a moment, grabbed the side of the boat, and propelled himself in. Another wave caught the boat and ripped it from the first mate's hand. He motioned for me to move closer to the edge of the rocks. Cold, wet, and scared, I stood there trembling while trying to keep my balance as the rowboat smashed into the rocks. Somehow, the first mate managed to get hold of the boat. He was holding the boat with one hand and pulling me forward with the other.

Jay was leaning out of the boat to reach for my hand as I inched forward. "Come on, you can do it," he shouted.

I tightened the straps on my life jacket, and with one large step I was off the rocks and fell into the boat. As Jay pulled me toward him, the first mate jumped from the rocky ledge and landed beside me. I clutched the seat beneath me.

The engine revved up and we headed toward the open ocean. The rowboat rocked and jumped as we approached the larger boat. At this point, I felt it was a safer place to be and was anxious to get on board.

With the help of the captain and the first mate, Jay and I settled onto the boat quickly. As we prepared to leave the area, a lone seal popped his head up near the boat. He studied us for a moment, and then suddenly disappeared beneath the waves.

For the next ninety minutes or so, the Captain maneuvered the boat through the rough seas. The crashing of the waves combined with the roar of the engine made it difficult to hold a conversation. So I sat quietly, clutching my camera equipment and peering out into the fog.

Slowly, the fog began to lifting to reveal hundreds of colorful buoys floating among the waves. They were marking the locations of the lobster pots beneath the surface. Gradually, the harbor came into view. Fishing boats rocked back and forth upon our approach. Near the rustic wooden piers, seagulls flew about calling to one another. Water pounded against the pilings while fisherman gathered to observe the sea conditions.

After thanking the captain and the first mate for returning us safely to the harbor, we climbed onto the pier. As we turned to wave goodbye, the sun began to peak through the fog and glisten on the turbulent water. I was quite relieved to be back on the shore, but I was disappointed at how brief our time on the island had been. In the morning, Jay and I would be heading home with our memories, and dozens of colorful images, planning out our next wildlife encounter.

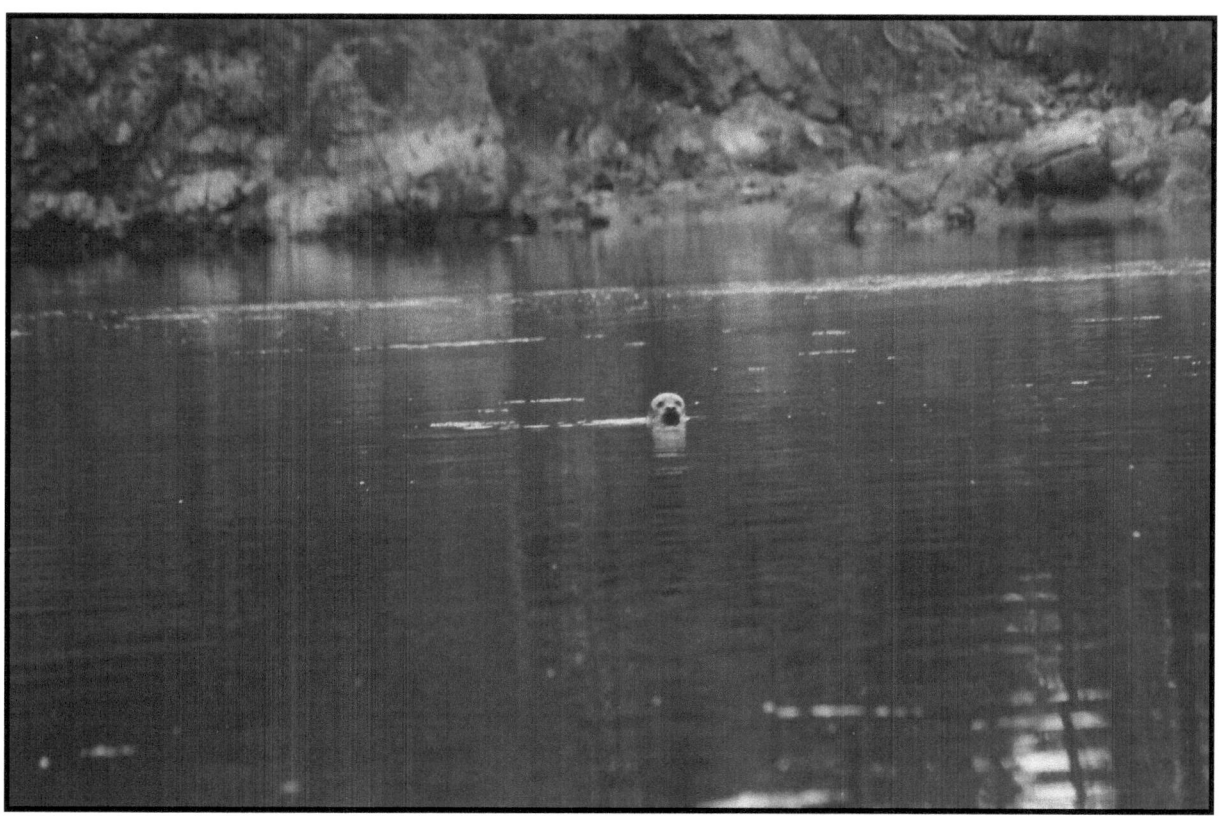

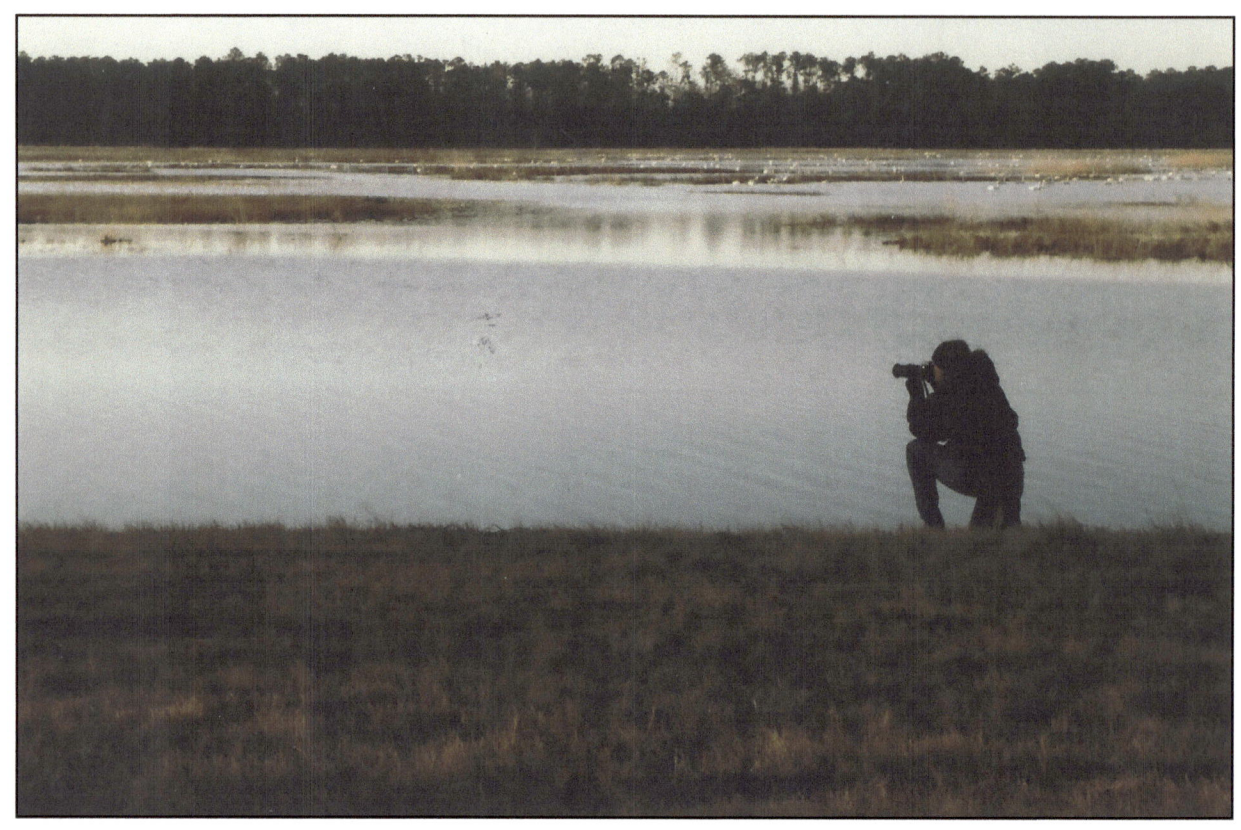

Message from S. J. Brown

In the numerous lectures I have given over the years, there are a few recurring questions I thought I should answer for my readers. One question I hear quite often is: What is my favorite animal? The answer is quite simple, the cooperative one right in front of the lens.

Another common question is: Have I ever been attacked by an animal?

As long as I keep in mind that I am visiting an animal's home and need to act accordingly, I stay out of harm's way. However, I occasionally get caught up in the encounter and forget this. That is when I tend to get in trouble. You should know that the animal kingdom has been tolerant with me and I still have all my fingers and toes.

Go to http://www.sjbrown.50megs.com/index.html for more information.